Contents

C000160615

Acknowledgements

In presenting this final report of the central team of the Joseph Rowntree Foundation Housing Finance Programme, I would like to record my gratitude to the Foundation for making such a major commitment to housing finance research over the last three years. Sir Donald Barron and Richard Best have shown a keen and continuing interest in the work of programme. Dr Janet Lewis, through a rare combination of diligence and diplomacy, co-ordinated the effective operation of the twenty or so projects in the programme.

The regional case study team leaders - Glen Bramley (Bristol), Steve Merrett (London), Roy Wilkinson and Tony Crook (Sheffield), Bruce Walker (Birmingham), Karen Hancock (Glasgow), Ken Willis and Stuart Cameron (Newcastle) - and their teams worked effectively and promptly; my task would have been impossible without them. John Hills, Christine Whitehead and Peter Kemp have all influenced my ideas on how to understand the housing finance system. Ken Gibb and Alison More, with computing support from John Malcolm, Mary Latham and Peter Lambie, have worked assiduously to produce this report. They all have my thanks.

Professor Duncan Maclennan,
Director
Joseph Rowntree Foundation Housing Finance Research Programme,
University of Glasgow.
April 1991.

Preface

*The Report **Paying for Britain's Housing** examined the major housing problems in six major conurbations. Problems of housing costs and conditions were concentrated in the rental sector, but not restricted to it. The bulk of poorly regarded housing, often in difficult neighbourhoods, was rented from councils. The report emphasised the major gaps in income and socio-economic status between the social and private housing sectors.*

It expressed concern that poorer, older owners apparently received little assistance and a growing proportion of well-to-do owners were encountering difficulties in repaying their mortgages.

Housing subsidy reform confronts two challenges. First, the creation of a regime for the rental sector which facilitates investment without putting an acceptable standard of housing beyond the incomes of low-income households; and, at the same time, secures value for money in housing investment and spending on services.

Second, the urgent priority to ensure that home-owners are also fairly subsidised; and that instability in house prices and interest rates do not unduly damage people's livelihoods, exacerbate regional differences and damage the potential growth of the national economy.

Assessment of actions to meet these challenges can be made by three criteria.

*Are the policies **fair**? Do households with similar incomes receive equal levels of support from government and do levels of assistance to the poor exceed those to the rich?*

*Are programmes **efficient**? Do they provide homes and services consistent with social objectives and the preferences of consumers? Are resources used with economy?*

*Do the policies help enhance economic **growth** without fuelling inflation?*

Preface

This report is concerned with the fairness, the efficiency and the growth aspects of housing policies; it examines the housing subsidy system at the end of the 1980s in Britain. Fairness has been a theme of British housing policy for almost a century and the 1980s saw an emphasis on efficiency, but the consequences for growth of housing policies has only appeared on the agenda of housing reformers or researchers in the 1990s.

Recent developments in British housing policy have emphasised the efficacy of 'individual choice'. If households, landlords or investors are really to shape choices, then assistance has to be neutral across tenures. Efficient and fair choices require a more level 'playing-field'. This must mean the avoidance of unlinked proposals for the reform of subsidies in the owned and rented sectors respectively; and the development of measures which are mutually supportive and span tenures. And it is important to recognise that such reforms may require gradual implementation.

There is not a 'unique' configuration of the housing system which is 'fair' and 'efficient'. Market failures of various kinds and the impact of housing on various social objectives may mean that policies are likely to be required other than those of 'competitive market prices' and 'housing allowances', even if the principles of the latter were to be the basis for a new, coherent finance system.

Research funded as part of the Joseph Rowntree Foundation's programme of work on the British housing finance system lies at the core of the report. The programme included local and national studies on specific topics and six local case studies in major conurbations which drew upon a specially commissioned survey of 10,000 households, the largest of its kind in Britain for over thirty years.

John Hills has recently published a report (1), which considered the fairness and efficiency aspects of the housing subsidy system. This report provides additional results, drawing upon the more detailed data available from the local case studies. The detail in the case studies is secured at the cost of national 'statistical' aggregation and this report should be read in the context of Hills' national estimates.

The first two chapters of the report set out the broad nature of changing finance and subsidy systems in Britain. Chapter 1 sets housing in the context of the national economy. The second chapter outlines major trends in public expenditure, particularly in the social rented sector. The next three chapters examine subsidy patterns in each of the main tenure sectors: council housing, the independent rented sector and owner-occupation. The final chapter considers reform of the present system.

Housing in the economy

Payments for housing in Britain commonly absorb 15 to 30 per cent of household budgets. Housing represents over half of the net wealth of British households; at the same time loans for housing make up two-thirds of their liabilities.

The construction industry employs close to one million people. Investment in the construction and renovation of housing is a fifth of gross investment in fixed capital in the economy; and it contributes over four per cent of national output.

The importance of housing in the national economy should therefore be obvious.

A common assumption has been that the housing market is 'driven' by economic change, especially incomes, interest rates and household formation, and in a predictable fashion. Housing progress depended on economic progress, even more so than economic development.

These views are now being urgently revised. There is a growing realisation that housing can transform or reinforce economic change with negative as well as positive results, feeding back into levels of inflation, expenditure and output. In short, the nature of the housing system influences prospects for economic growth.

At the same time, there is growing recognition that British housing subsidy and policy arrangements encourage house price inflation; and that rising house prices can boost inflation rates not only by fuelling wage claims but by encouraging higher levels of consumer expenditure. The success of any reforms of the housing finance system will depend on whether they curtail such processes and, at the same time, break the pattern of high interest rates, mortgage arrears and repossessions experienced in Britain during the past two years.

This chapter examines these issues in detail. The cases for reform on the basis of equity and efficiency have been made for decades, but the macro-economic argument is a recent one. The next section sets out a summary of key features of the UK housing market. The third considers the range of factors which triggered and ended the boom of the 1980s. The fourth section outlines the consequences of the boom, especially the nature and importance of equity withdrawal. The concluding section sets out the likely scenario for the economy into the 1990s and measures which could ameliorate matters.

Patterns into the 1990s

The 'boom-and-bust' phenomenon in the national housing market from 1986 to 1991 has been, in many respects, typical of the last two decades. In a recent paper Fleming and Nellis **(1)** produced a comprehensive analysis of the anatomy of house price cycles in Britain over the period 1969 to 1989. (See **Figure 1**)

Between 1969 to 1989 the money value of average house prices rose by a factor of 15, just over twice the

Figure 1

Annual percentage changes in nominal house prices, quarter on quarter, 1969 Q1 - 1990 Q1, UK

Source: Fleming, M.C. and Nellis, J.G. op. cit, p. 35

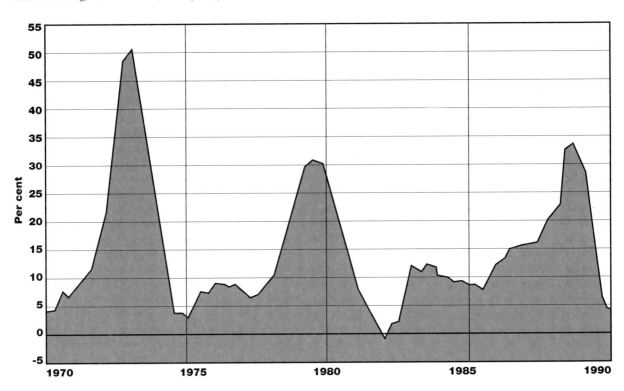

expansion rate of the Retail Price Index. This doubling in the real value of dwellings and the increase in home ownership from 50 per cent to 67 per cent meant that housing asset growth comprised two thirds of the doubling in household wealth during this period. The difference between home values and outstanding mortgage debt, the personal sector's housing asset base, had reached £750 billion by 1988.

The progression in asset values was neither smooth over time nor across the regional housing markets of the country. Three booms in housing prices have occurred in the last two decades: in 1971-73, 1978-80 and 1987-89. Each boom was followed by a 'bust' period, but prior to 1989 the trough periods did not generate a fall in house prices, except in the first quarter of 1982. The current trough has been more prolonged than its predecessors: starting in late 1988, it is now expected to end in mid-1991. Further, nominal price falls, at around 3 per cent on average, occurred for 1990; in southern regions of Britain house prices have fallen by a fifth since 1988.

The regional pattern of house price inflation displayed major variations in the overall expansion rate and in the extent and timing of instability. For instance, from 1969 to 1989 prices in the South-East expanded by a factor of 17, and in Northern Ireland by 7. Coombes and Raybould (2) have examined the period 1984-1989 in detail across 280 local labour markets. These were their broad conclusions:

- All but 37 of 280 local housing markets experienced a surge of price inflation between 1984 and 1989.
- Inflation rates varied markedly within regions as well as across them.
- Southern housing markets responded first to the expansionary pressures.
- Where such expansion took place, the surge was less pronounced and less certain in northern regions.

A variety of inter-regional connections can spread price pressures rising initially in southern Britain to more remote regions: households relocating to the North, extended long-distance commuting, employees transferring with plants away from the areas where congestion creates higher costs; all these factors have an impact. And, of course, where rising house prices in the South induce wage increases (3), then comparable wage-setting across regions may raise the potential pressure for higher incomes in the North.

Housing markets have an inevitable local dimension. There is a growing body of evidence that disparities in such regional price appreciation hamper labour mobility between regions and reinforce regional differences in wealth.

Asset formation through house-price rises and equity withdrawal of these gains played a critical role in the recent boom; this is explained further below. The housing asset gains observed in the six local case studies are shown in **Table 1**. It shows how prices rose from 1983 to 1988 after standardising for the characteristics of dwellings traded in each year, see Appendix 1. For instance, house prices in Birmingham were £19,036 lower in 1987 than in 1988. The figures suggest that, in 1987-88, major proportional increases occurred in Birmingham, Bristol and Sheffield, that they were insignificant in Glasgow and Newcastle and that London gains had been more pronounced in the previous year. These figures emphasise both the regional variations in the large shifts in wealth and in the timing of the gains. A single 'macro' policy instrument, in particular the interest rate, may be a crude tool for dealing with regions experiencing a very different set of pressures.

Table 1

House price differences between 1988 and 1983 in the case study areas (£)

Area	Birmingham	Bristol	Glasgow	London	Newcastle	Sheffield
1983	-31336	-39924	-11582	-60938	-8424	-13438
1984	-24749	-34769	-9795	-44622	-8631	-17215
1985	-27574	-34749	-7357	-45729	-3060	-13447
1986	-23088	-31001	nsd	-22770	-2662	-13138
1987	-19036	-19726	nsd	-7653	-1034	-9640
Average house price						
1987	36159	49559	36210	86154	30454	29758
1988	51229	66164	38803	104197	31691	36369

nsd=not significantly different

See Appendix for details of the standardisation procedures.

Explaining booms and busts

Housing booms end as house prices rise relative to incomes and demand-limiting influences finally outweigh expectations of house-price rises, at least as long as wage rates do not rise fully to offset house-price increases. Before financial deregulation, when there was an element of building society rationing of mortgages, then in inflationary periods rising interest rates rose ahead of mortgage rates. This reduced inflows of funds to societies and encouraging them to increase deposit requirements from home-buyers, thus further stabilising demand.

With the removal of restrictions (the 'corset') on bank lending in 1980, the banks rapidly expanded mortgage lending: by 79 per cent in 1981 and 109 per cent in 1982. A series of responses occurred in the building society movement. The mortgage rate 'cartel' terminated, the terms and conditions of lending were eased and growing recourse to wholesale funding was made to sustain lending when retail market flows moved against societies.

Financial deregulation appears to have had a number of consequences. At the end of 1989, the average ratio of loans to prices did not fall back significantly from the high levels which had emerged in the decade. Between 1982-1988, household borrowing became more geared in relation to incomes. At the start of the period, the ratio of financial liabilities to income for the average household was 0.56 and by the end 1.11. It is difficult to envisage this gearing ratio rising in the 1990s. High 'gearing' facilitates purchase in the price upswing, but leaves consumers exposed in the down-turn. The ratio of initial mortgage repayment to average earnings (for the average loan) was 24 per cent in the 1972 peak, 30 per cent in 1980 but rose to 51 per cent in 1990.

Although gross and net housing wealth values were increasing to 1988, mortgage liabilities were also expanding. Between 1981 and 1988 the share of housing loans in all household liabilities rose from 58 to 66 per cent; during that period "the rapid growth of loans for house purchase accounts for virtually the entire increase in financial liabilities as a percentage of net wealth" (4). Outstanding mortgage debt rose as a percentage of the asset value of dwellings from 20 to 28 per cent from 1981 to 1988.

The Bank of England, in a perceptive comparison with other advanced economies (5), indicates that the macro-economic gearing ratio of Mortgage Debt/GDP rose from 32 to 58 per cent over the period 1982 to 1989. In 1989, comparable rates were 45 per cent (USA),

22 per cent (Germany), 21 per cent France and 25 per cent (Japan).

The housing finance systems in these other countries, which are generally open to deregulatory pressures, require owners to find a substantial deposit sum. Aside from reducing collective and individual exposure to gearing, such measures increase the savings rate and boost the stock demand for rental (usually private) housing. Tax systems, finance arrangements and destructive rental sector policies in Britain have guided young Britons into early, often frenzied and increasingly debt-encumbered routes into owner-occupation (6). This is not just a feature of 1986-1989, or even the 'Thatcher years', but of the last two decades. Financial deregulation may well have mattered, therefore, in the last boom, insofar as traditional non-price rationing of loan/deposit ratios was de-emphasised, thus removing an important damping mechanism. But it is also clear that increased credit volumes flowed into a housing system which tended to transform expenditure into price rises rather than output (7).

Housing Construction

The cyclical 'bust' periods may also have systematic causes. On the demand side, 'frenzy' effects may induce some of the potential entrants to the housing market to accelerate their purchase of homes, thus reducing the subsequent flow of demand. But the key influences occur on the supply side. Housing production in Britain, reflecting lags attributable to firms as well as the planning system, commonly takes two years to respond to price signals and thus fuels the 'boom' and reinforces the 'bust'. Peak output, often occurs after the peak in real prices; and, with unsold stocks of units, developers quickly reduce output and employment, thus exacerbating the economic down-turn.

The British housing construction industry has undergone a number of major changes in the 1980s (8). Until the down-turn in the housing market after 1988, the housing sector had been increasing its share of all construction activity (from 39 per cent to 42 per cent in the period 1980-88). This was against a background of a long-term decline in the volume of new housing output, which had averaged 300,000 units per annum in the 1960s, 250,000 in the 1970s and 200,000 per annum in the 1980s.

Within the total of new building, private sector activity has progressively displaced public building of housing. At the start of the 1980s, the public sector started around 40 per cent of dwellings but by 1989 this share had fallen to just over 10 per cent. New housing output has, in effect, become increasingly driven by market factors; this has arguably made housing output shift more in line with the general economic cycle than previously.

The long-term downward shift in new housing construction has been offset by a major expansion in the value of repair and improvement work, especially in the public sector. In the 1980s, such work has increased its share from half to almost two-thirds of residential construction. This growth, combined with the long recovery in pri-vate starts from 1983 to 1988, explains why the residential sector grew faster and with greater stability than overall construction to 1988. Since then, new

Table 2

Private sector housing land prices by region: 1988 levels and 1988 index numbers based on 1985 = 100

	£ per plot	Simple average £000 per hectare	Median £ per plot	£000 per per hectare	Price index
North	5394	101	432	69	162
Yorks and Humber	4513	111	3132	86	112
East Midlands	10934	252	8085	187	244
East Anglia	21528	420	20617	327	336
Greater London	55325	2438	26841	2471	304
South East, excl. Greater London	39959	896	32246	705	271
Outer Metropolitan	50305	1083	46584	1041	275
Outer South East	30540	712	26235	554	266
South West	15428	385	10758	278	226
West Midlands	11819	311	4755	173	214
North West	6475	130	5863	158	143
Wales	5298	115	3363	83	184
England & South Wales	18170	427	9223	200	252

Source: Department of Environment: Housing and Construction Statistics 1979-89

building has plummeted: 1991 has been a year of bankruptcy in the industry and has seen what is likely to be the lowest level of housing output since 1914.

Construction costs, excluding land, fluctuated in the early 1980s, experiencing sharp falls in 1981 and sustained increases since 1984. Real land costs, prior to the 1988 bust, also rose sharply in the period 1985-88. **Table 2**, based on an analysis by the Sheffield project team, indicates the sharp rise in land prices for housing especially in the South.

The case study teams probed, where possible, the relationship between changes in house prices and shifts in new private construction. At the local scale, there are often no clear patterns linking prices and output. The Bristol team, who stressed the problems of drawing robust conclusions from the data, attempted to estimate the responsiveness of housing starts to price changes (the elasticity of the supply of housing) for the Bristol area and Great Britain. The measured supply elasticities for the Bristol area were 0.2, 1.3 and 2.1 allowing for responses, respectively, with no lags, within a year and within 2 years. The national estimates were lower (for 1 and 2 years) at 0.57 and 0.48. The evidence may be 'fuzzy' and sensitive to assumptions but all the estimates confirm the unresponsiveness of housing supply to changing prices. In consequence, rapid growth in demand stimulates house and land prices and this inevitably means that a proportion of tax subsidies raises housing prices.

At any time, the supply of vacancies on the housing market reflects not just new stock but vacancies advertised by existing owners either moving or intending to move. From 1978 to 1988, the number of units traded on the UK housing market, at least those requiring loans, doubled from 800,000 to 1,600,000 (excluding new construction for the private sector; these figures are 640,000 and 1,400,000). The equivalent figures for the end of 1989 were 900,000 (750,000). For the majority of moves are local in nature and can be postponed until trading conditions improve. In the new construction sector, developers with land banks, with similar expectations, rationally curtail output quickly. These factors contribute to the 'ratchet' effect on Britain's housing prices, which raises real prices rapidly in 'boom' periods but ensures more modest real price falls in the down-turn.

The recent cycle and equity withdrawal

House-price cycles are not, therefore, a new phenomenon in the British economy. There is, however, evidence that a number of factors, including changing financial regulations and practices, have altered the ways in which housing prices have an impact upon the economy. Since the mid-1980s, it has been recognised that 'equity withdrawal' from the housing market can have important, sometimes adverse consequences for the control of the economy.

Rising real house prices can influence household spending in a number of ways. They include:

- increasing the value of housing inheritances, the vast majority of which are sold;
- the retention of part of the net proceeds by movers selling and buying;
- remortgaging, extending loans etc against rising values of houses by households staying put;
- encouraging greater spending and less saving by households who feel wealthier because they occupy more expensive houses.

The research programme examined the first three of these effects, both in a special study and using the data from the local case studies.

Lowe and Watson (9) produced national estimates of equity withdrawal by inheritors, movers and 'last-time sellers'. They concluded that equity withdrawal had reached £16.4 billion per annum in 1988 (contrasting with less than a billion a decade earlier), thereby adding 2 per cent to national spending power.

Extraction of equity on moving (£10.8 billion) and inheritance (£6 billion) were the major sources of withdrawal. The overall estimate of withdrawal recorded by Lowe accords closely with the gap between the increase in mortgages and values of additions to the owner-occupied stock calculated by Costello and Coles (10). They report a total of £16.8bn.

The household survey data from the case studies was used to identify how rising housing values influenced consumer borrowing as a source of equity withdrawal.

The capacity of individuals to withdraw equity is a function both of the rate of house-price appreciation and the length of time over which houses have been held. Two thirds of 1988/89 owners had owned their current house before 1985. A third had bought before 1975 and a tenth before 1960. As real house prices have risen over the last two decades by 1.5 per cent per annum, the real gains have been considerable.

There are important regional variations in gains (see **Table 2**). Over the period 1978-88, 37 per cent of

Table 3:

Home-owners in 1989

Motives for financial rearrangement (grouped): 1970-88

	Mortgage Replacement	Additional Loan	Mortgage Supplemented
Buy other Home	3.1	2.7	-
Extend House	25.1	18.9	24.1
Repair or Improve	43.5	56.3	58.7
Switch to Endowment	17.9	nr	nr
Business Investment	6.3	10.2	4.2
Non-Housing	21.5	21.6	8.6
Buy-out Spouse	5.8	1.5	6.8

N=303   N=403   N=555

nr=not relevant

Table 4

Home-owners in 1989

Additional borrowing and expenditure on improvement 1984-88 (current prices)

	A Mean value of spending on improvement	**B** Mean new loan	**A/B**
1984	5419	20111	27
1985	6163	11040	56
1986	4918	12350	40
1987	5453	11820	46
1988	4227	14840	28

owners in the three northern regions had either replaced or supplemented mortgages or taken additional loans. In the southern regions, this proportion rose to 67 per cent.

Households undertaking such activities were most likely to be over 55 years of age (in 1988) and least likely to be under 30. By 1988, pre-1975 purchasers had 'borrowed' 15 per cent of their past gains, purchasers in the period 1976-82 some 25 per cent and post-1982 purchasers about 18 per cent.

The major years of withdrawal by borrowing were 1985 and 1987. The results suggest that there was a 'backlogging' effect with pre-1982 gains stored in housing values until financial deregulation began to have an impact. The mean loan amount extracted was, in 1988 prices, of the order of £9000. The sources of these loans were markedly different from first loans; only 42 per cent were granted by building societies and the major lenders were banks, often overseas banks with a London base.

However, it is important not to equate all loans with equity withdrawal from housing. Rising house prices may encourage households to extend their homes, using loan finance, rather than move. And, as home-owners are not always regular maintainers of property, loans may be used to pay for capitalised repairs as well as major redecoration and improvement.

The household survey probed the reasons non-movers gave for taking loans and, importantly, independently checked whether they had spent money on their housing in the period 1983-1988. Respondents claimed that around three-quarters of borrowing was for 'housing' purposes (see **Table 3**). But, for the 1983-1988 period, the survey data indicated that less than half the value of supposedly housing loans was used for repairs and/or improvement and extension of homes (see **Table 4**). This implies that more than half of additional borrowing against housing asset values left the housing sector. However, it would be wrong to suggest that all of it entered consumption: households indicated that some 7 per cent of borrowing was for 'business' purposes and at least some of the remainder may have gone to the purchase of alternative assets such as shares, or even been deposited in building societies.

It was apparent from the timing of equity withdrawal by households that past gains were not the sole stimulus to refinancing. The majority of households borrowing above mean amounts (more than £9000) did so to restore their outstanding loan debt back to the £30,000 limit of mortgage interest tax relief; that is, until new restrictions introduced in the 1988 Budget, a household could essentially secure tax-subsidised loans up to a loan limit of £30,000 by remortgaging . In this respect, MITR was inefficient in two senses: first, it subsidised expenditure on non-housing items if loans were used in the non-housing sector; second, any effects of MITR on prices may eventually have leaked into the economy in general.

The extent of additional borrowing against housing asset values means that national estimates of the extent of equity withdrawal may be understated. The survey indicates the pervasive use of banks for additional loans, and these loans may not be formal mortgages although dwelling values may have been regarded both as an encouragement by the consumer to purchase and by institutions to lend. In crude terms, such borrowing could have comprised a quarter of all additional borrowing, implying withdrawal of £2.5 billion in 1988 and £3 billion in 1990. This would boost estimates of overall withdrawal to £23.8 billion in 1988 and £16.9 billion in 1990.

These very provisional estimates of withdrawal based upon refinancing behaviour suggest that it has a magnitude of greater scale than previously realised; and that it may be more stable than the equity withdrawal of 'movers' studied by Lowe. The further implication is that withdrawal may have been half as large again as previous estimates suggested. However, these figures are tentative; the sample is not 'national' and further investigation is required before they are given the firmness of the components identified by Lowe.

Beyond the boom

Rising house prices in the boom created damaging economic pressures apart from the consequences of equity withdrawal. Rising house prices raised rents in the private sector and land and construction costs for the social sector. Rising rents and house prices create pressures for higher wages.

General increases in interest rates were the key policy instruments chosen to curtail the economy in 1989 and 1990. High interest rates helped sustain the value of sterling, now in the context of the ERM, which is otherwise damaged by rising imports caused by UK consumption. And as the Government perceived the link between growing housing wealth and consumption, increased mortgage rates became a route to restraining growth in housing asset values and of reducing non-mortgage spending as interest repayments rose.

Between mid-1988 and mid-1990, UK interest rates rose from 8.5 to 15 per cent with inevitable consequences for first-time buyers' (raising initial mortgage payment-to-income ratios from 31 per cent in January 1988 to 51 per cent in January 1990). Subsequent reductions in interest rates reduced this ratio to around 40 per cent by January 1991. In 1990-91, real income in the UK fell by 2 per cent, house prices have reduced in real terms and the volume of output and transactions have slumped. At the time of writing it is expected that real income in the UK will grow by 2 per cent in 1991-92 and that interest rates could fall as far as 11 per cent by the end of 1991. It is widely agreed that 1991 and 1992 will be years of steady recovery in the housing market rather than an accelerating boom.

In the context of this recovery there are, however, two nagging and unanswered questions. First, what rate of house-price appreciation represents 'steady' recovery? And when real prices recover, will the growth in housing equity destabilise consumption again? The Chancellor, in the 1991 Budget speech, introduced removal of higher tax rate relief on mortgage interest payments with a reference to the need to avoid a house-price boom. And in the following week the Governor of the Bank of England, who had eschewed the use of credit controls in the 1980s, reflected the Bank's unease about such booms when he told the Treasury Select Committee: "I am attracted by the idea of some sort of restriction on levels of lending for individual mortgages". These concerns are well placed, though the wrong policy solution may have been identified, if the economic forecasts for 1990 to 1993 are examined.

However with a target inflation rate of 4 per cent and interest rates in the range from 11.5 per cent to 13 per cent, macro-economic models are forecasting real house-price increases, such as those in **Figure 2** based upon the Oxford Economic Forecasting Model.

Some commentators (**10**) have argued that the last boom was unusual and was fuelled by:

- sustained high real income growth of 4 - 5 per cent per annum from 1986-88;
- a 'once-for-all' effect of financial deregulation;
- unusually loose monetary policy following the stock market slump in 1987;
- cuts in the income tax rate in 1988 from 60 to 40 per cent for high-income earners and from 27 to 25 per cent for others in 1988;
- the gap of five months between the announcement and implementation of the ending of 'double' tax relief for two adults jointly purchasing a dwelling.

These points have substance. The programme research

suggests that a one per cent increase in disposable income will, in the medium term, raise real house prices by 0.3 and 0.4 per cent.

The extent to which these initially gentle upward pressures on house prices become the next boom, and how far that boom refuels equity withdrawal, will depend upon what has changed over the last five years and how the 1990s will differ from the 1980s.

Will the 1990s be different?

It is unlikely that housing demand growth will be as rapid between 1991 and 1996 as it was between 1984 and 1989. John Ermisch (11) has indicated clearly that rates of household formation will fall sharply towards the end of the decade. Real income growth, at least in the first half of the decade, is not likely to exceed 2 – 3 per cent, and therefore lie well below the second half of the 1980s.

Figure 2

House prices - annual percentage change
Source: Independent on Sunday 10.3.91

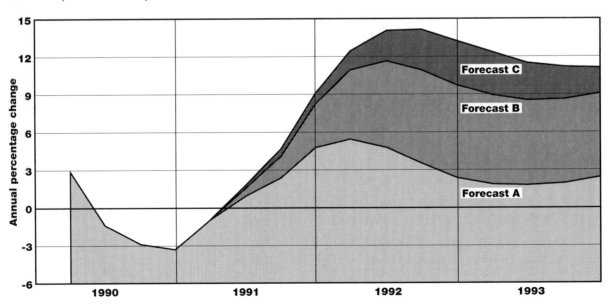

Tax changes are likely to reduce the favourable subsidy status of purchasers. The removal of tax relief at the higher tax rate and the non-indexation of the £30,000 limit are signs that the Government is predisposed to gradual reductions in the per capita value of tax reliefs for owner-occupation. The Chancellor's hope that the removal of higher rate tax relief will have a major dampening impact on inflation may be optimistic: past experience suggests that price pressures start in the first-time buyer market. The reintroduction of a property tax as a basis for local government finance is further likely to reduce demand by prospective home-owners, especially in the upper quarter of the market. (See chapter 5).

Demand side behaviour may also be influenced by the experience of the recent down-turn in housing prices. Individuals, particularly those inclined to a highly geared borrowing position, may now recognise the riskiness of housing investment; and lending institutions cannot be satisfied with the current rates of mortgage arrears and repossessions.

In the context of ERM, and perhaps ultimately EMU, British mortgage rates will have to respond to interest rate policies aimed at external stability rather than affordability by home-owners. This problem will not disappear: high and sharply variable rates may dominate the 1990s. These rates, other things remaining equal, could be as much as 2 per cent lower by the mid 1990s if MITR were to be phased out by 1995.

The broad supply structure of British housing has not changed since the last boom. There are no reasons to believe that, without a major shift in policy, the construction sector will respond differently in the 1990s. Indeed, land pressures may increase with new importance attached to environmental concerns; and the male-dominated nature of the construction sector is likely to be associated with labour shortages in the industry as the labour market tightens.

If there is a price boom, equity withdrawal is likely to expand. Tax changes in the 1988 Budget may have assuaged the tendency to withdraw to top-up tax relief and the 'backlog' factor will be much less pronounced. With the net value of housing assets still in excess of £700 billion and beginning to rise, it would be foolish to assume that consumption will not be affected. Policies must aim to minimise real house-price increases.

Policy developments

If the broad structural pattern of demand, supply, finance and taxation remain much as they are at present, there is likely to be a price boom before the late 1990s. In the early recovery phase, government could adopt a number of housing policy measures which could exert pressures towards constant real house prices and minimise the damaging effects of price rises. Key measures are set out below.

1   The Government should accelerate, for macro-economic reasons, the removal of the favourable tax status of owner-occupation. A capital gains tax on housing is unlikely to be politically feasible in Britain (see Chapter 5) in the 1990s.

A simulation of the effects of removing MITR has been undertaken by Steve Wilcox (12) using the Treasury model (11). A phased abolition of MITR by 1995-1996 would reduce consumer spending, GDP and house prices, *ceteris paribus*. However, if the gain in tax revenues were to reduce the PSBR/PSDR, interest rates could be 2 per cent less than at present and would largely eliminate the deflationary effects of MITR removal. These simulations, and alternatives, are reported in more detail elsewhere and their 'micro' consequences are considered in Chapter 5.

2   There is a case for considering a more neutral tax regime between owned and private rented housing, especially until MITR is reduced. This would adapt the supply of housing, as in our European competitors, to provide rental units for younger households who could abandon 'frenzied' buying behaviour in booms and accumulate first-time-buyer deposits in an economic environment where house-price appreciation rates do not outstrip the rate of interest on their deposits.

3   A purposeful approach has to be adopted to housing construction which recognises the tensions of macro-economic policy, housing output and environmental quality. Appropriate and sustained training in the construction sector is required. Above all there should be a major review of how planning authorities plan land release and adapt to local price increases.

4   Capital adequacy rules for financing housing investment, in all sectors, need to be looked at afresh.

5   The Government has to pay more attention to the urban and regional patterns of economic growth, and how they are influenced by transport, regional and housing policies. In the 1980s. the Govern-

ment placed less emphasis on regional economic policies and, given the forms of assistance used, there may have been a strong case for this. However, disregard for the costs of congestion, and house-price rises in particular (so that the indicator of difficulty was taken to be a sign of success), has meant that the long-run growth/inflation trade-off confronting the British economy is less favourable than it could be. A new approach would require a much more purposeful consideration of the kind of urban and regional Britain the government wants for the 21st century.

One approach would be to gear linked investment in housing, the environment and transport towards locations with surplus land and labour, as long as labour productivity in such places was not inherently lower. The experience of Glasgow in the 1980s illustrates this approach. The alternative is to crowd growth into southern Britain and, if costs and subsidies are not to rise, relax land zoning to secure growth with stable house prices. There would be obvious environmental effects of such a policy which may be inappropriate to the mood of the 1990s.

6 These policy measures aim to 'neutralise' the favoured tax position of home-ownership. They are aimed at creating a more economically efficient, price-sensitive housing system. Such a thrust to policy is preferable to a reintroduction of credit rationing or re-regulation in the housing finance sector.

The high gearing rates of UK home buyers undoubtedly contribute to price booms and to the difficulties of households in arrears and facing repossession. But lending restrictions, which will be particularly onerous for first-time buyers, should only be contemplated if government fails of reform the housing market and if financial institutions and individuals have not learned from the most recent bust. Failure to reform will mean that the Governor of the Bank of England and individual commentators (13) have a strong case for re-regulation.

Broader Concerns

Shifts in interest rates, taxation and house prices have their most obvious effects in the owner-occupied market. And this is especially true for first-time buyers where some policy development would be required were MITR to be abolished. But more stable and lower house-price levels in the future would also have major implications for the rental sector. Both social and private rental tenants are now more directly influenced by such factors than in the past. Rising house prices and property values, in a deregulated rental market, are swiftly translated into rent increases, with capital gains accruing to landlords.

With rents in the council sector now influenced by 'sales-market values' in the ring-fencing regime, the council sector is now required to adapt more rapidly to changing house prices. Rising land costs are quickly felt in the expanding housing association sector and (unlike the council sector with now 100 per cent subsidy on interest charges for new council housing) rising interest rates ration off the number of projects which are both affordable and privately financed. All of this argues for a general economic framework with relatively stable prices and a tendency to constant real house prices.

Rising real prices and/or interest rates leads to higher 'market-value rents' and a widening of the subsidy gap between 'social' and market sectors; this increases housing benefit bills and precludes the political possibility of harmonising property-pricing in the owned and rental sectors. The programme research indicates that the gap between actual and market rents fell in most places between 1985-1987. The house price boom of 1987-89 re-opened the gap, though

rising rents and static prices in 1990-91 have substantially narrowed the gap. The present period offers a major opportunity to ensure that the gap disappears.

The hiatus in demand for housing of the early 1990s gives government the opportunity to rethink the framework of the supply side which would ensure efficient use of finance and subsidies in a market-oriented housing system. It is to these subsidies that the report turns in the next chapters.

The Government's declared aim is "to ensure an adequate supply of housing at subsidised rents for the diminishing proportion of households who cannot afford the market price of decent housing" (1). There is room for debate over the terms 'adequate', 'afford' and 'decent' and whether the Government is likely to meet its objectives in these areas.

Public Spending: the process outlined

For at least 15 years the announcement of public spending programmes for housing have been greeted with less than enthusiasm by the major housing lobbies. An image of housing spending in the 1980s has emerged which suggests a saga of unending cuts: a caricature of relentless reductions in current subsidies, of escalation in council rents greater than rises in inflation and earnings, of drastic curtailment of capital investment, of deterioration in the quality of services and of the Housing Corporation and housing associations being treated better than local authorities.

This image is only true of some programmes and in some places. In particular, the key feature of public spending on housing is that, following major reductions to 1982, there have not been real cutbacks on a major scale, but rather a marked restructuring of capital programmes and current account subsidies.

Overall Changes in Spending

By the mid 1970s, General Government Expenditure absorbed almost half of national income. Strict monetary policies, privatisation and a range of other policies were introduced after 1979 to reduce public expenditure. However, during the 1980s, public spending has persistently risen in real terms; in most areas of expenditure cutback targets were not achieved. Growth in public spending has been outstripped by expansion in incomes, especially in the period 1985-89. In consequence, the ratio of public spending to national income fell from 47.5 to 39.5 between 1983 to 1989 and has subsequently remained relatively stable. This sharp reduction was achieved by freezing real government spending through a period when real GDP grew by 18 per cent.

Public spending on housing, unlike many other areas of public expenditure, was sharply curtailed in the early 1980s. During the period 1979-80 to 1982-83, housing programmes 'contributed' three quarters of all spending cuts and the housing share of public spending fell from 5.8 to 2.3 per cent (2). The rapidity and severity of this cut-back reflected the capital-intensive nature of housing (as capital programmes can be more readily curtailed than recurrent subsidies), the Government's faith in the efficacy of market solutions, the deferred nature of the consequences of housing cut-backs and, perhaps, the inability of the housing industry to articulate a new case for housing investment.

During the longer period 1976 to 1989, the housing share of central government spending (the Planning Total in the Financial Statement) fell from 11 per cent to 3.5 per cent of the total. The future outlook for housing within this total seems forlorn: although real spending in total is expected to grow by 1.75 per cent per annum to 1994, the housing share is to fall from 3.8 in 1990/91 to 3.3 in 1993/94.

Table 5

Public spending on housing 1976/77 to 1989/90, £ billion at 1988/89 prices (a)

	Current (GB)	Net capital (GB)	Current plus net capital (UK)	Housing benefit (b) (UK)	Total public spending (UK)	Mortgage interest relief (c) (UK)
1976/77	3.9	8.3	12.7	2.2	14.8	3.4
1977/78	3.5	6.5	10.4	2.2	12.6	2.9
1978/79	3.8	5.7	9.9	2.1	12.0	2.7
1979/80	4.3	6.0	10.7	1.9	12.1	3.1
1980/81	4.1	4.5	9.0	2.0	11.1	3.5
1981/82	2.9	2.8	6.1	3.0	9.0	3.4
1982/83	2.2	2.6	5.1	3.5	8.7	3.3
1983/84	1.8	3.5	5.6	3.4	9.1	3.6
1984/85	1.7	3.3	5.4	3.8	9.2	4.4
1985/86	1.7	2.7	4.7	3.8	8.7	5.5
1986/87	1.7	2.4	4.4	4.1	8.6	5.3
1987/88	1.6	2.3	4.3	4.2	8.5	5.2
1988/89	1.4	1.2	3.0	4.1	7.0	5.5
1989/90	1.5	1.5	3.3	4.2	7.5	6.5

Notes:

(a) Adjusted by GDP deflector

(b) On current definitions

(c) Including Option Mortgage Subsidy until 1983/84

Sources: HM Treasury (1990), Tables 8.1, 8.2, 15.1, 15.2, 16.1, 16.2, 17.1, 21.2.1, 21.2.9, F1, and earlier equivalents;

Welsh Office (1989), Table 9.1 and earlier equivalents;

Scottish Development Department (1990), Table 15.5, and earlier equivalents;

Board of Inland Revenue (1989). Table 5.1; Official Report 12 March 1990, cois WA93-96.

Although the planning totals may convey something about housing claims on central government revenues, they actually tell us very little about housing spending by public bodies. These totals exclude activities financed from the revenues and sales receipts of public housing organisations, mainly local authorities and the housing quangos, and private sector contributions.

John Hills (3) has produced a series of estimates for real public spending on housing from 1976 to 1989 and they are reproduced in **Table 5**. These figures also net out spending financed by sales receipts and other revenues, and this is particularly important in relation to capital spending.

Measured in net terms, real capital spending in 1989 was only 18 per cent of its 1976 total. But the comparable statistics are 56 per cent for real gross capital spending (including spending based on receipts) and 63 per cent for volume-adjusted spending (where gross capital spending is deflated by the building cost index).

The differences between gross and net totals largely reflect the increasing share of capital receipts in funding housing programmes. This proportion grew steadily from 7 per cent in 1979 and by 1989 receipts paid for 70 per cent of spending by councils in England (and around 30 per cent in Scotland). This reliance on receipts, which have fallen in real terms in the two years since 1989, raises a key question about how net Planning Totals for capital spending are to be boosted in the future.

Capital spending:
Changes by time and place

Change in capital expenditure has differed by time, location and programmes. Real cutbacks in capital spending were largely confined to the period 1979 to 1982. In the period since 1985, capital spending has been relatively constant in real terms, but with a major rise in 1988/89 as sales receipts were unexpectedly large. A second important point is that although the share of gross spending undertaken by the quangos (primarily funded from the Planning Total, or net capital spending) increased sharply in England, Scotland and Wales in the early 1980s, their relative share of gross spending fell over the period 1985-89 (to under a quarter in England and Scotland and to a third in Wales).

Both of these observations contradict the common caricature. In the latter half of the 1980s, real gross spending remained relatively constant and housing associations did not receive a marked increase in the share of investment but rather a reduction (see chapter 4). Ironically, this was precisely the period when Government came to regard the housing associations as the leading edge for providing social housing in future. This sentiment has been translated into programme spending only after 1990 and only really in England and Wales. The housing association movement in Scotland is now facing a near standstill public-spending budget.

Regional differences

There have been significant regional variations in real capital spending. By 1989, England still spent less than in 1982, Scotland about the same and Wales had experienced significant growth. These differences primarily reflect the powers of virement of the Secretaries of State for Scotland and Wales for increasing spending on housing within the limits of their block grants. And they attached greater priority to housing policy than Department of Environment Housing Ministers in the 1980s.

As part of the Foundation's housing finance programme Mark Kleinman examined the changing pattern of gross capital expenditure by local authorities and the Housing Corporation in England, Wales and Scotland (local authorities only). Over the period 1980-86 (the period of major change), half of English local authorities experienced a real growth in spending and the comparable figures for Scotland and Wales were 55 and 57 per cent respectively.

The change in relative fortunes was not random across England. Real local authority capital expenditure rose by a fifth in East Anglia, the South-East and the South-West but fell by a quarter in London, the North and the North-West (where authorities must have regarded events in the rather similar housing contexts of Scotland and Wales with some interest).

The changes also favoured rural rather than urban areas. Spending in the conurbations fell by a fifth, but rose by 5 per cent in small towns and 10 per cent in rural areas. Kleinman also indicated that much of this shifting pattern was unrelated to 'need' but rather reflected higher sales rates and prices in more prosperous regions. In brief, the reliance on sales receipts resulted in gross investment patterns which neither favoured the Government's preferred sector (housing associations) nor channelled resources to the areas in greatest need.

In Greater London, for the decade 1979-89, central government capital spending permissions (HIPs) fell as a share of the English total from 35 per cent to 32 per cent and in real terms by 58 per cent. But overall spending fell by 46 per cent. As HIPs fell, local authorities increased permitted sales receipt spending and spending on non-prescribed items (not counted against overall capital spending - chiefly capitalised housing repairs). They also became involved in leasing, creative accounting and land deals with housing associations and private developers. In Greater London, by 1988/89, capital spending was funded by £382 million capital receipts, and £249 million of non-prescribed expenditure, plus a HIP of £370 million.

In some areas real spending expanded markedly even as HIPs fell. In the Bristol case study area, where capital spending by local authorities trebled in the 1980s, the HIP fell from four-fifths to a quarter of the total over the same period. Experience varied not only across, but within regions. In the Sheffield study, two of the authorities sustained capital programme increases but in three others real spending was halved.

Growth in renovation

The local case studies illustrated the incentives (through non-prescribed capitalised repairs) to expand renovation. In London, renovation of existing council stock rose from 31 to 66 per cent of capital and building of new houses by local authorities fell from 43 to 14 per cent. The comparable figures in the other studies are similar.

The switch within programme headings was, however, consistent with policy objectives. Hills has shown that, in the period 1976 to 1989, although new building by

local authorities fell by 90 per cent, renovation almost doubled. The changing pattern for the 1980s in England also occurred in Scotland and Wales and by the end of the decade almost two-thirds of local authority spending was devoted to renovation programmes.

This shift in output raises an important point. Many, if not all, programmes have a role in urban regeneration, but this wider role of housing gets little mention in PES papers and has not been at the forefront of lobby arguments. When estimating the value of subsidies and designing subsidy systems, critics have concentrated on the benefits of policies on individuals and on 'affordability' rather than on the wider benefits of programmes, so ignoring what are called 'externalities'. There are few convincing estimates of their size: how does spending on housing renovation reduce unemployment, lower local crime rates, facilitate private investment or lessen health service costs by reducing dampness? The consequence is that the contemporary case for housing investment and the potential role of producer subsidies is often understated.

There has been a growing tendency since the early 1980s for Government to earmark capital spending for specific purposes, in contrast to the block grant arrangements introduced in the late 1970s, and in spite of local authorities switching spending in line with government spending. By 1990, expenditure grants for specific purposes, such as 'Estate Action' or Homelessness, comprised almost a quarter of local authority programmes.

New rules for capital spending

At the end of the 1980s, central government recognised some of the limitations of targeting capital programmes and introduced new financial regimes for housing associations (throughout Britain) and for local authorities (but not in Scotland).

The importance of sales receipts was one of the factors prompting the change in England and Wales. After 1981/82, councils had been allowed to spend a pre-scribed proportion of their receipts, though this proportion fell from 50 to 20 per cent as receipts outstripped Government willingness to allow councils to allocate them to housing. The prescribed proportion was not restricted in Scotland. Authorities were also allowed to spend the prescribed proportion of receipts of accumulated unused sales revenues from previous years in addition to 'in-year' receipts, this process being known as 'cascading'. By 1989, £8 billion of receipts were waiting to cascade. The capital budget available to local authorities consisted of the range of sources illustrated for London on pages 26 - 27.

From the fiscal year 1990/91, local authorities are to have a tripartite budget. The Basic Credit Approval (BCA) (£1,445 million in England in 1990-91) is a borrowing permission given to each local authority, taking into account likely sales receipts (and in this way government is free to re-allocate the Planning Total to 'needier' authorities and, of course, the Housing Corporation). The second component is net sales receipts, though future debt repayment and contributions towards funding rent rebates are now deducted, plus other net revenues (thus allowing rent surpluses to fund investment). This sum is expected to exceed BCA in 1990/91 (running at £1,688 million). The third component is Specific Credit Approvals, that is borrowing permitted for specific forms of investment favoured by the Government. Apart from facilitating the redistribution of sales receipts, the new system also extends the planning period from one to three years.

Current account spending

After 1980-81, the Government sharply reduced revenue subsidies to Housing Revenue Accounts. Previously, this subsidy (called Housing Subsidy in England and Wales and called Housing Support Grant in Scotland) had been the main instrument for reducing housing costs faced by council tenants.

Table 6 shows the movements over the decade from 1979-80 in central government expenditure on Housing Subsidy and Housing Support Grant in real terms.

The biggest reduction was in 1981-82, but the downward trend continued, so that in 1989 these subsidies were less than a fifth of their real value a decade ago. In addition, there was a contraction in the number of local authorities receiving subsidy. In 1989, fewer than

Table 6

Housing Subsidy and Housing Support Grant in real terms 1979-80 to 1989-90

	England & Wales	Scotland
1979-80	100	100
1980-81	95	90
1981-82	54	58
1982-83	29	35
1983-84	15	23
1984-85	17	21
1985-86	19	19
1986-87	24	13
1987-88	20	11
1988-89	19	14
1989-90	19	15

Sources: Government Expenditure Plans, cmnds. 9143 and 288, and Hansard, 15 July 1988, cols. 399-400 and cmnd. 1508 (February 1991).

one in five local authorities in England and Wales received housing subsidy, compared to 95 per cent in 1981-82.

The result of these changes in expenditure on subsidies was a shift in the regional impact of Housing Subsidy and Housing Support Grant. This is shown in **Table 7**. Between 1981-82 and 1987-88, there was a large increase in the proportion of total grant going to the London boroughs, from 41 per cent to 70 per cent. The only other region to maintain something close to its earlier share was the North-West. Scotland's share of the total subsidy has halved from 15 per cent to 8 per cent.

Another consequence of the reductions in subsidies to Housing Revenue Accounts was the restructuring of the HRA, as shown in **Table 8**. Housing subsidy in England and Wales covered just 8 per cent of Housing Revenue Account expenditure in 1987-88 compared to almost a third in 1980-81. Faced with falling subsidies and rising costs, local authorities could either increase rents or increase the level of contributions made from the general rate fund to the Housing Revenue Account. Since the Government was anxious to restrict the growth of overall local authority spending, penalties and restrictions curtailed the use of rate fund

Public expenditure cuts and changes

Table 7

Regional distribution of Housing Subsidy
and Housing Support Grant

	1981-82 %	1987-88 %
Northern	4.4	2.3
Yorkshire & Humberside	4.6	0.1
East Midlands	3.6	2.1
Eastern	4.7	2.0
London	41.3	69.6
South-East	6.7	4.7
South West	2.3	0.6
West Midlands	6.2	1.9
North-West	7.8	6.5
Wales	3.3	2.0
Scotland	15.1	8.1
	100.0	100.0

Sources: CIPFA Housing Revenue Account Statistics and Hansard, 15 July 1988, cols. 399-400.

Table 8

Structure of the Housing Revenue Account
in England and Wales

	1980-81 %	1987-88 %
Revenue:		
Rents	48	68
Rate fund contribution	10	8
Exchequer subsidy	32	8
Interest on unspent capital receipts	5	11
Other income	5	6
	100	100
Expenditure:		
Loan interest and repayments	66	51
Repair and maintenance	20	27
Supervision and management	12	19
Other expenditure	2	2
Transfer to rate fund	0	1
	100	100

Source: Maclennan and Kearns, 1990

contributions (RFCs), so that they covered only 8 per cent of HRA expenditure in Great Britain in 1987-88 compared to 15 per cent in 1984.

By 1989-90, almost 70 per cent of HRA expenditure was met by rental income. Rents on council housing in Britain rose rapidly in the first half of the decade, and the overall real increase from 1979 to 1989 was close to a half. Real income growth, at least for those on average earnings (though the proportion of social housing tenants enjoying such levels is small) has also been sustained; the ratio of council rents to average earnings is now around 10 per cent, compared with 7 per cent in 1980.

Restrictions on the proportion of receipts from council house sales which may be reinvested in housing meant that annual interest on those receipts covered over 10 per cent of HRA expenditure by 1989 and indirectly reduced housing benefit subsidy to council tenants.

The curtailment of local authority investment in new council housing over the past decade and the growing reliance upon receipts has resulted in the proportion of income devoted to repayments of capital and interest on loans falling from two-thirds in 1980-81 to one half in 1987-88.

The gain has been in the amounts of income spent on management and maintenance: 19 per cent and 27 per cent respectively in England and Wales in 1987-88. Between 1980 and 1985 the real expenditure per dwelling on management and maintenance rose by 50 per cent and 35 per cent respectively. John Hills estimates that real management and maintenance spending per dwelling has grown by 4.8 per cent per annum since 1976.

Rising rents may have implied increases in rent-to-income ratios for tenants not receiving state benefits (4). However,

Table 9

Central government expenditure on rent rebates to council tenants

Cash Index in Real Terms	(£000)	(1988 prices)
1983-84	1,980	100
1984-85	2,145	103
1985-86	2,294	104
1986-87	2,421	106
1987-88	2,563	108
1988-89	2,720	108
1989-90	2,800	111
1990-91	3,000	119

Source: Government Supply Estimates

although Housing Subsidy and Rate Fund contributions were progressively reducing, it was housing benefit rather than personal incomes which paid rent increases for benefit recipients. Housing benefit has become the main source of assistance with housing costs through the 1980s. Whilst Housing Subsidy and Housing Support Grant totalled little over £500 million in 1989, central government expenditure on rent rebates (that part of the housing benefit system then applicable to council tenants) was close to £3 billion. Indeed, the cost of administering the housing benefit system was approximately half the amount of Housing Subsidy in 1988/89. See **Table 9**.

In real terms, total spending on rent rebates to council tenants has been rising; by 1987-88 around 54 per cent of council tenants in Great Britain received an average rebate of £790 per year. Assuming the average housing benefit recipient pays the average council rent, then rent rebates cover 60 per cent of the costs of providing housing services to those council tenants in receipt of housing benefit, who numbered 3.37 million tenants in 1988-89 (5).

Table 10

Regional distribution of Rent Rebate Subsidy 1987-88

Local authority	£m	%	%
Northern	178.6	8.3	7.6
Yorkshire & Humberside	237.2	11.1	12.6
East Midlands	144.3	6.7	7.8
Eastern	155.5	7.3	9.6
London	330.9	15.4	17.1
South-East	252.4	11.8	9.9
South-West	147.1	6.9	7.1
West Midlands	262.8	12.3	7.8
North-West	313.7	14.7	15.3
Wales	117.6	5.5	5.2
	2140.1	100.0	100.0

Source: CIPFA Housing Revenue Account Statistics

Table 10 shows the regional distribution of housing benefit subsidy paid into Housing Revenue Accounts in 1987-88 and compares this to the regional distribution of local authority dwellings in the same year. The two distributions are remarkably similar, apart from the fact that the South-East and the West Midlands have much higher shares of the rent rebate subsidy than their shares of the total number of local authority dwellings. In particular, the West Midlands had 8 per cent of council housing but received 12 per cent of the housing benefit subsidy. Given that council tenants in the West Midlands are not that much poorer than council tenants elsewhere (6), this pattern arises either because tenants in some areas were paying for the recent construction or renovation of their homes (and hence facing higher interest charges), or because some councils chose to charge higher rents in order to provide a better service or because councils imposed 'monopolistic' rent increases. (The pattern in the local studies is reported in chapter 3).

New rules for current spending

By the end of the 1980s, the structure and size of the different subsidies flowing to council tenants caused the Government concern for two reasons. First, the diminishing wedge of combined housing subsidy and Rate Fund Contributions meant that central government could no longer ensure annual rent increases by withdrawing subsidy; too many authorities were 'free' of subsidy influence. Secondly, the burgeoning housing benefit bill implied that rent increases progressively manifested themselves in Social Security spending funded by the Government.

The Government responded by introducing, at the start of fiscal year 1990/1991, a new regime for local authority housing subsidies which has come to be known as the 'ring-fence system'. Its main features are a tighter definition of the Housing Revenue Account which prohibits transfers between the HRA and other accounts of the local authority, and the introduction of Housing Revenue Account Subsidy to replace the range of current subsidies into the HRA, namely Housing Subsidy, rate fund contributions supported by Rate Support Grant and the rent-rebate element of housing benefit subsidy.

In constructing the 'notional' Revenue Account for assessing Housing Subsidy, the Department of the Environment is using new allowance rates for management and maintenance spending and linking local guideline rent increases to local house-price changes, but with a minimum and maximum rise to dampen rent changes.

There have been a number of immediate effects of these changes on the Housing Revenue Account. Council housing will have to 'stand on its feet' more than before, and in particular its costs must have no effect on the size of the community charge and its replacement (the council tax). Although Rate Fund Contributions made up only 8 per cent of the total income to the aggregate HRA in England and Wales in 1987-88, in some authorities the discretionary RFC was very significant in covering HRA expenditure. Of all local authorities in England and Wales, 194 made contributions from the General Rate Fund to the HRA in 1987-88, and 126 made transfers from the HRA to the General Rate Fund.

A further, medium-term effect is that rent increases related to capital values, at the level of the local authority, may give some coherence to council rents. The redefinition of housing subsidy creates a new and greater 'wedge' of revenue controlled by Government in the HRA, with a share of the 'notional' HRA of just over 40 per cent for 1990-91. The Government has re-established control over local current accounts.

An extension and reprise

While subsidies to the HRA fell, housing benefit rose and there was an almost constant real annual expenditure on their combined total of around £6 billion.

Further, the magnitudes of housing benefit and other subsidies barely changed between 1985 and 1989. Throughout this period there was a changing number of tenants. Using 1988/89 prices, combined 'current' and housing benefit spending per tenant actually rose by over 10 per cent between 1984 and 1989. For much of the period, the real budget of the Housing Corporation was stable. (See chapter 4).

Real trends in mortgage interest tax relief are also set out in **Table 5**. Accepting MITR as the main cash flow measure of subsidy to owners, Hills charts the growth of MITR from £3.5 million to £6.5 million between 1976/77 and 1989/90. The sum of current spending, housing benefit and MITR, rose from £9.5 billion in 1976/77 to £11.5 billion in 1984/85 and to £12.2 billion by 1989/90. Overall cash-flow subsidies to housing in Britain have been increasing, especially in the second half of the 1980s, and they have increased by 2 per cent per house since 1984/85.

Restructuring has been extensive: until the mid-1980s, there were sustained shifts from 'bricks-and-mortar' to 'personal' subsidies, and from the rented sector to owner-occupation. If there remains a genuine concern about the overall level of public spending on capital compared with the past, the real issues regarding current spending are with the distribution of subsidies and their influence on the operational efficiency of markets and public authorities in providing housing and housing services.

The adequacy of public expenditure planning

Government Spending Plan statements and Departmental Reports follow the conventions of Government accounting. There is no doubt that the format and content of the Autumn Statement is helpful for grasping the broad effect of housing programmes on government finances. However, it is much less clear that the Statement, and associated Departmental Reports, which are the Government's only annual review of the housing system and plans to change it, provide useful information about the impact of government spending on housing investment and subsidies.

Through the 1980s the Government has advocated notions of 'economy', 'efficiency', 'targeting', 'private leverage' and so on, in housing as well as other areas. The inadequacies of local authority and housing association accounts for assessing 'effectiveness' have been stressed elsewhere (7), and indeed by Government. But how well do the PES-related statements address such questions regarding the national housing effort?

A number of concerns about the PES system are well known. Planning totals are stated in cash terms; there may be sound anti-inflation policy reasons for this, but past out-turn figures could be stated in real and volume terms without damaging this objective (and Departmental Reports now include some 'real' figures). Capital and current spending are lumped together. The annual character of plans, with only aggregate totals projected forwards in cash terms, is also problematic for a sector largely producing capital goods; it implies commitments and carry-forward between financial years. A broad breakdown between carry-forward and new investment for each major programme would give a better understanding of the impact of programmes on the housing industry.

There is also room for debate on how 'public' is defined in the public expenditure accounts, especially in relation to capital spending. Consider the following illustration.

A private landlord funds a renovation project with a 45 per cent improvement grant and lets the housing with half of revenues over the life-time of the project paid by housing benefit. A council landlord funding a similar project could have no capital grant, Housing Revenue Account subsidies of 20 per cent and again half of gross rents paid by housing benefit. In the public spending accounts all of the council investment would be treated as 'public' spending and only 45 per cent of the private landlord's project would be so attributed. But over the life of the project the private landlords' level of subsidy will be greater, and indeed the council may sell the house, so creating a receipt.

Departmental Reports, at least, should separate three considerations. First, there should be an indication of the likely 'current' subsidies accruing in the future as a result of capital spending. Second, the extent to which the 'public' status guarantees project returns needs to be considered. But this would be better measured by the implicit or explicit costs of 'insuring' public spending projects against default rather than assuming they equate to all capital spending totals. A third point is the rate of interest at which the capital is raised. It is obvious that capital raised through the government sector will have a lower risk premium, given government guarantees against default.

But, as has been demonstrated recently in the housing association sector, there may also be economies of scale and reduced transaction costs where government raises funds directly. The PES capital statement, unless it is to be solely concerned with PSBR or PSDR, should state the subsidy implications, insurance premiums and interest rates at which capital is raised.

Post-1987 experience in the housing association sector has indicated a Treasury willingness to be flexible on such matters. Before then, as for councils, all capital spending was classed as 'public'. With the introduction of the new financial regime for associations after 1989, all residual loans privately financed could be regarded as 'private' rather than public, even if the public Housing Association Grant component was 90 per cent or over. In seeking a more level playing-field in the rental sector, it has to be recognised that the present PES system is not even-handed in favouring private over social investment (at any given subsidy rate) and associations over councils.

The absence of an asset account for the housing sector, in particular council-related activities, not only inhibits an understanding of the consequences of privatisation but precludes any understanding of the rate of return being earned in the social housing sector and, by implication, any economic measure of subsidies.

In recent years, annual Departmental Reports accompanying the Autumn Statement have produced much

useful information. But changes are needed. The inconsistent coverage of Reports for England, Scotland and Wales, for instance, makes difficult the calculation of even basic statistics for Great Britain, such as housing construction activity by sector in 1989/90.

There are more fundamental omissions. The changing regional distribution of capital spending could easily be included as a supplementary table, with local authority and association investment compared and contrasted. If a value-for-money ethos was indeed being adopted, the reports should set out the objectives for 'territorial allocation' and the outcomes for public capital; and they should indicate the distribution formulae for associations and councils.

In the future, public spending through associations and an expanded, enabling role for councils is intended to 'lever in' increased private investment. Current reports duck this issue; they seem stuck with a pre-1980s conception of the role of government in the housing sector. Public spending plans for housing should include, for each major programme, an estimate of likely leverage and expected output levels.

Reports also contain little flavour of the outputs produced from spending on housing: numbers of units or renovations are as far as they go. But in a contemporary view of what housing is and does in the economy and society, such figures could be regarded as no more than mere restatements of inputs. Housing spending, as noted earlier, is important not only because it provides shelter; it renovates neighbourhoods, reduces health care costs, and has an impact on the environment.

But some practical limits have to be set. For major programmes, however, it should be essential to describe the impact of programmes on neighbourhood renewal, cities, the environment and the economy. If the Government will not do this, it has a conception of housing which is outmoded and different from tenants, let alone academics. If it cannot do this, and this is possible as there are no more than half-a-dozen economists in the Government service working on housing issues, then housing spending is not well grounded in fact and analysis.

If Housing Ministers cannot stress the importance of housing in the national economy, in creating healthy environments and cities worth living in, then they will be easy meat in the lions' den of the PES Star Chamber. During the last decade, ministers have demolished spending programmes which they

regarded as not serving the nation's long-term interest. But, other than in the area of tenure change, they have struggled to create a coherent replacement for the role of British housing policy.

Analysts (8) have estimated that 60,000 units of new social housing per annum will be required in Great Britain during the 1990s and that modernisation of social housing may require £30 billion of investment spread over the period. Meeting these needs requires a better understanding of how housing investment shapes households' economic opportunities if the claims of housing for scarce public resources are to be met.

'Ring-fencing' chaos?

Reforming subsidies for council houses

A decade ago, critics of council housing subsidies could point to the significant proportion of middle-income groups who rented extensively subsidised council homes. **Paying for Britain's Housing** *emphasised that by 1989 council housing was predominantly rented by poor households; there are stark contrasts with owner-occupation.*

Although better targeting of subsidies remains a valid concern, the overall level of support for council housing is the fundamental issue. Efficient reforms must avoid further impoverishment of the sector. This chapter examines present patterns of subsidy across and within the case-study authorities. Alternative pricing policies are examined and a new approach based on capital value rents suggested.

A housing subsidy, as defined in this report, constitutes the gap between the competitive market price of housing and the rent actually paid by a household. The extent of this gap in the council sector depends not only upon cash-flow subsidies (Housing Subsidy, Rate Fund Contributions etc) and housing benefit payments but also upon the pricing systems and accounting rules used within the council sector.

Local adjustment: diversity or disarray?

Funding of council housing is managed within the Housing Revenue Account (see Chapter 2). After 1980, authorities were required to make the account balance or run at a surplus. Until the introduction of 'ring-fencing' in 1990, authorities could transfer surpluses out of the account for use in other local spending activities or they could make discretionary payments to the account from local tax revenues. From 1980 to 1990, they were also allowed to use the annual interest receipts from past, unspent sales receipts to defray HRA expenditure.

Within the HRA the costs and revenues of all housing projects are 'pooled' into a single account. Flows of revenue are required to repay the principal on housing loans. However, this principal is measured in historic costs; capital outstanding is not indexed for inflation nor for increasing replacement costs. In periods of sustained inflation, historic-cost pricing offers a potential means of assuaging price increases (increasing subsidies).

Historic-cost pricing and multiple-funding sources gave councils a range of rent-setting options for protection against inflation and reductions in Housing Subsidy. The subsequent disarray emerged not from local ignorance but as a result of local government choices in the face of complex central government incentives and penalties (1). Responsibility for the patterns described below lies in the corridors of Whitehall as well as in town halls.

Adjustment in the 1980s

After 1980, reductions in Housing Subsidy and the requirement to avoid HRA deficits did not, as indicated in chapter 2, lead to reductions in HRA expenditure. As real expenditures rose, councils, reacting to DoE incentives, first raised then lowered RFCs and increased rents. By the end of 1989 almost half of authorities earned HRA surpluses.

The real increase in rents of almost 50 per cent occurred in Scotland as well as in England and Wales, though the systems of control were different. Within all three countries, however, local authorities reacted differently to the changing subsidy levels and rules. In Greater London, the average real rent increase from 1979 to 1988 was 42 per cent. But this varied from moderate increases in Brent (13 per cent) and Bexley (25 per cent) to large increases in Wandsworth (123 per cent), and Croydon (93 per cent). At the other end of the country, around Glasgow, affluent Eastwood had constant real rents whereas they doubled in nearby, deprived Clydebank.

The experience in the Sheffield case-study area after 1982/83 illustrated well the range of local choices made even where Housing Subsidy was no longer paid. After 1982/83, none of the authorities received Housing Subsidy. Three of the five chose to make zero or minimal RFC contributions. Sheffield City took the decision to pay an RFC supposedly set equal to the amount local owner-occupiers would, on average, receive from MITR. Rotherham decided, after 1982/83, not to raise rents at all.

This diversity in rents could be defended on the basis of local government responding with sensitivity to local preferences; this is as important as acting as a local agent for central government policies. Against this view, however, there are two major considerations: national policies regarding tenure choice can be offset by local rent policy choices. More importantly, local discretion was largely funded upon the back of housing benefit which was, in the 1980s, predominantly funded by national tax revenues.

Some authorities quickly recognised that 'dependent' tenants would not pay rent increases but have them largely offset by housing benefit payments. The variety

Table 11

Benefits as a proportion of gross income, 1982/3 - 1987/8

	1982/3	1983/4	1984/5	1985/6	1986/7	1987/8
Sheffield	12.2	48.3	54.8	59.0	59.6	60.1
Rotherham	24.4	50.8	55.9	33.8	54.0	52.3
High Peak	15.9	49.6	51.5	52.1	51.3	50.4
N E Derbyshire	21.7	43.2	50.5	44.9	44.9	44.6
Derbyshire Dales	15.1	43.8	56.2	56.9	59.1	45.3

Source: CIPFA HRA Statistics

of the share of housing benefit in gross rent payments for the Sheffield authorities is indicated in **Table 11** and similar patterns were reported in all the local case-study areas (see Appendix 2). Variation in this proportion reflected differences in local rent-level choices more than differences in local client groups. This pattern is not consistent with an efficient use of housing benefit and diversity meant disarray in subsidy provision.

Authorities not only have some discretion about average rent levels but they have discretion over the ways in which rents are set on individual dwellings. The pricing pattern is examined below.

Pricing within the case-study areas

This report makes reference to 'hedonic' house prices (see Appendix 1). This is a statistical technique to assess which characteristics of properties affect their prices. When it is applied to owner-occupied homes, a few key characteristics commonly explain at least half of the variation in house prices.

The extent to which there was systematic rent-setting in the council stock of the case-study areas was examined by relating gross rents (before housing benefit payments) to property characteristics. In the Glasgow, Sheffield, Birmingham and Newcastle regions, property character-istics explained only a quarter of the variation in gross rents. In London this fell to 16 per cent and Bristol 11 per cent. In Newcastle and Sheffield, where there were complex points schemes for rent-setting in the larger districts, the highest 'explanations' of rents in terms of their property characteristics (26 and 27 per cent) were observed. This suggests that even complex rent schemes can fail to match gross rents and property characteristics in a consistent fashion.

Within the case-study regions, individual local authorities were confronted with different configurations of their Housing Revenue Accounts and made different choices.

When 'district' effects were included in the analysis of gross rents, London levels of explanation increased but were still low; Glasgow and Newcastle all rose; and in Bristol and Birmingham the pattern remained the same. In general, the tests never explained more than a third of the variation in gross rents observed in the household survey, considerably lower than similar 'explanations' for the owner-occupied market. The pricing of council housing is clearly in disarray within British conurbations; this immediately calls into question the fairness and efficiency of subsidies in the system. (For comparisons with the independent rental sector see chapter 4).

Subsidies to council tenants

The local case-study teams examined concepts of subsidy and measured 'break-even' (cash-flow subsidies balancing the HRA) and 'market-value'-based estimates of subsidy.

Examples and explanations of these approaches are reported in Bramley et al (2). This chapter examines market-value-based estimates of council subsidies.

The estimates assumed that rents included an annual expenditure of £420 on management and maintenance and an allowance for depreciation at 1 per cent per annum of the estimated market value of the dwelling (3). The rents derived below assumed that a chosen rate of return is earned net of those costs.

The rates of return used were given in real terms. Property returns consist of two components: appreciation in asset values and rental income. Both components were included in the required rates, unless stated otherwise, and housing capital-gain rates were derived from the Department of Environment 5 per cent sample of mortgages for the relevant regions over the period 1968-1989.

Two rates of return were employed. First, following the Duke of Edinburgh's Inquiry of 1985, a 4 per cent rate of return was specified. Second, a 5.5 per cent rate was also used as this reflected the real long-term return to non-residential property in Britain over the last two decades.

The rate of return was applied to a capital valuation. Because council stock is not traded in an open market,

Table 12

Estimated market values in local authority and housing association sectors

Regions	Full-market Values		Bottom-half Values	
	LA	HA	LA	HA
Birmingham	22486	30618	26306	26542
Bristol	35731	31599	31580	29064
Glasgow	28391	33248	28498	26760
London	70278	71781	34534	33407
Newcastle	17635	17120	24913	23559
Sheffield	18301	19479	24157	24374

Right-to-Buy sales are a selective sample of it; and because resale values of council housing sold on the market are not widely available, the market value of council properties has to be estimated or imputed. For each of the case-study regions, property-valuation weights were derived by relating owner-occupied dwelling characteristics to sale prices, (see Appendix 1). These weights, derived from the market as a whole, were then applied to the characteristics of individual council properties in each region.

However, within each regional housing market, it is likely that the incomes and preferences of social sector residents are more similar to those of households residing in the lower-value segments of the housing market. If the present stock of council housing were to be sold *in toto*, the level and structure of prices would probably be very different from the market average. Therefore, a second set of pricing weights was estimated, based on the bottom half of each regional market. (Ideally the weights should have been estimated for the lowest quarter of the owner-occupied market, but the number of cases available precluded this exercise.)

The average 'full-market' and 'bottom-half' values of rented housing are presented in **Table 12**. On average, the 'bottom-half' valuation produced lower values than the 'full-market' basis, but the pattern differed by region. Values for Bristol and especially London were sharply reduced, those for Glasgow and Birmingham remained relatively stable, and those for Sheffield and Newcastle actually increased; (some 'characteristics' may be more expensive in lower-value markets).

If the approach to pricing council housing advocated below is taken seriously as an option for policy reform, then it needs to be repeated with larger samples using computerised house-price databases. The principles employed are sound and the patterns observed for Southern Britain enhance the feasibility of reforms.

- Estimated market rents. Market-rent levels using a variety of rates of return, capital-gain rates and market valuations of housing are set out in **Table 13**.

- Rents based on a 5.5 per cent rate of return and full-market values, allowing no capital gains, would produce daunting rent increases, tripling in London, Bristol and Glasgow. Gross rents based upon these values would absorb most of the income of almost two-thirds of council tenants. They do not form the basis for a feasible reform.

Table 13

Gross rents, net rents and ranges of market rents for council housing

| | Actual Rents 1989 | | No Capital Gain | | | Capital Gain % | | Market | |
| | | | Full-market Value (1) | bottom-half Value | Full-market Value | Local Gain Rates Full market | bottom half | Value Gap (2) % | |
	Gross Rent	Net Rent	(5.5)	(4.0)	(4.0)	(5.5)	(4.0)	1989	1991
Birmingham	1011	564	1933	1845	1568	1546	1440	36	16
Bristol	967	579	2825	2131	2202	1529	1157	56	48
Glasgow	829	495	2369	1964	1837	2007	1669	55	79
London	1176	801	5194	2292	3936	2526	1196	70	58
Newcastle	1045	522	1634	1754	1322	1191	1250	21	5
Sheffield	1037	551	1651	1729	1342	1068	1063	23	1

(1) Figures in brackets are the rates of return applied.
(2) Based on full-market values with a 4 per cent rate of return.
The gap is measured as (market-value rents - gross rents) divided by market-value rents.

'Ring-fencing' chaos?

- Rents based on a 4 per cent return on full-market values, again with no capital gain allowed, would result in the 'market-value gaps' for 1989, as indicated in the second last column of **Table 13**. These gaps range from 20 per cent in Sheffield and Newcastle, through over 50 per cent in Bristol and Glasgow to 70 per cent in London. If it is recalled that it took ten years for government to raise real rents by 50 per cent, from 1979 to 1989, this pricing criterion does not seem to be a reasonable basis for reform.

- Pricing based on a 5.5 per cent return on full-market values but allowing for local capital gains would generate small rent increases in Newcastle and Sheffield but rises in excess of 50 per cent in Bristol and Birmingham and over 100 per cent in London and Glasgow.

- Since 1990, 'ring-fencing' has been associated with marked rent increases and market values of properties have declined. Such changes, incorporated into the analysis by indexing rents and house prices in

Table 14

Estimated market rents, rents and subsidies by region.

	1 (a)	**2**	**3** (b)	**4**	**5** (c)	**6** (d)
			Rent gap as a			All subsidies as
	Estimated	Actual	percentage of actual	Actual	Estimated subsidy	a proportion of
	market rent	gross rent	gross rent (%)	net rent	per tenant	market rents (%)
Birmingham	1440	1011	42	564	876	61
Bristol	1157	969	19	579	578	50
Glasgow	1669	829	101	495	1174	70
London	1197	1176	2	801	396	33
Newcastle	1254	1046	20	522	732	58
Sheffield	1063	1037	3	551	512	48

(a) Based on a 4% return, bottom half values and allowing local capital gains.

(b) Column 3 = (column 1 – column 2) divided by column 2.

(c) Column 5 = column 1 – column 4.

(d) Column 6 = column 5 divided by column 1.

real terms, suggest that the market gaps on full-market values with a 4 per cent return have fallen; (see final column, **Table 13**). The exception is Glasgow, which lies outside the ring-fencing regime. But the substantial gaps remaining in Bristol and London imply difficulties in using this pricing criterion across the country.

- 'Bottom-half' values, 4 per cent returns including capital gains do produce a more feasible set of rents; (see **Table 14**). In England, only Birmingham, with a gap between market and current rents at 42 per cent, raises major difficulties, although Glasgow, with a doubling of rents required, remains problematic.

This last rent-setting criterion, which we believe to have the most appropriate capital values, was analysed in more detail and subsidy measures based upon it examined, but concern remains over the low London estimate. (Although the absolute values of subsidies would be larger with other pricing criteria, the relative patterns by household income, age etc would remain unchanged.)

The broad patterns arising from the '4 per cent, capital-gain-included, bottom-half' estimates of rents are indicated in **Table 14**. The contribution of actual payments of rents by tenants (current net rents) ranges from 67 per cent in London to 30 per cent in Glasgow. This implies, conversely, that subsidies as a proportion of estimated market rents arising from rent distortions, Housing Subsidy, Rate Fund Contributions and housing benefit ranged from 70 per cent in Glasgow to 33 per cent in London. And in the other areas, they amounted to between 50 and 60 per cent. Properly measured, council subsidies are still very extensive.

This pricing rule still does not form a likely basis for badly-needed reform. However the pattern of subsidies it generates is displayed in **Tables 15** and **16**.

Subsidy patterns

Subsidies to tenants can be sub-divided into rent distortion effects and housing benefit payments. The value of gross and net (including housing benefit) subsidies are illustrated for Glasgow, Bristol and Sheffield by different income groups. Rent distortion subsidies are low (even negative for upper-income tenants) in Sheffield, moderate in Bristol and high in Glasgow.

The rent-distortion subsidies (**Table 15** column 1) are relatively constant across all income groups in all

Table 15
Rent subsidies, housing benefit and household income

Gross Household Income	Market Rent Minus Gross Rent	Market Rent Minus Net Rent	Gross Rent/ Market Rent
Glasgow			
< 2,600	907	1483	0.45
2,600-5,199	858	1324	0.48
5,200-7,199	834	1117	0.50
7,800-10,399	792	814	0.52
10,400-13,999	813	844	0.53
14,000-15,599	829	829	0.52
15,600-20,800	763	763	0.55
Bristol			
< 2,600	215	864	0.81
2,600-5,199	184	758	0.84
5,200-7,199	151	365	0.87
7,800-10,399	213	278	0.82
10,400-13,999	152	152	0.87
Sheffield			
< 2600	53	846	0.95
2,600-5,199	35	656	0.97
5,200-7,199	5	258	1.00
7,800-10,399	25	54	0.98
10,400-13,999	-12	30	1.01
14,000-15,599	-76	-76	1.07

regions, with a tendency to be marginally lower for tenants in the middle-income bands. Housing benefit makes the distribution of overall subsidies strongly progressive up to incomes of £7,200, after which there is a sharp drop in subsidy received. Above this figure the distribution is mildly progressive as higher income tenants receive lower rent-distortion benefits.

Average values of subsidies (including housing benefit) were estimated by white/non white status, household age and location. The results are shown in **Table 16**. The average subsidy for non-whites (£467) is considerably less than for whites (£782). As both groups receive similar housing benefit levels, these differences arise from local pricing policies and the geographic pattern of non-white households. Younger and older households receive higher subsidies than do households aged 35-39, and this primarily reflects housing benefit.

Satisfied and dissatisfied tenants pay similar levels of gross rent. However, very dissatisfied tenants receive significantly higher subsidy levels both through rent distortions and housing benefit.

Moving forward
The discussion so far has established a dilemma: rents are disordered across and within local authorities and

Table 16

Council housing subsidies by selected socio-economic variables
(Lower market values, 4 per cent, local capital gain)

	Number of cases	Mean subsidy	Standard deviation
Age of head of household			
16-24	169	931	647
25-34	423	783	542
35-44	373	697	545
45-59	600	693	552
60+	1222	803	468
Ethnic status			
White	2689	782	509
Non-white	113	467	753
Distance from city centre			
< 5 km	1320	727	512
5.01 - 10	915	797	552
10.01 - 15	382	866	498
15.01 - 20	136	699	537
> 20	61	788	456
Satisfaction with accommodation			
Very satisfied	687	757	540
Satisfied	1366	748	532
Neither	358	826	502
Dissatisfied	266	774	493
Very dissatisfied	127	902	504

this issue requires resolution to ensure fair subsidies and the efficient use of housing benefit. However, even the most gentle pricing regime examined above, 4 per cent (allowing for local capital gains) applied to lower market values, leaves large gaps between 'market' and actual rents.

The problems of using this pricing criterion are exacerbated by the likelihood that gains in property prices may be lower in the 1990s than in the 1980s, which means that required rent levels may be closer to the 'no-capital-gain' estimates. Indeed, as a search for more stable house prices is central to our argument for a reduction in mortgage interest tax relief, it would be illogical to argue that the capital-gain element in rates of return will be high in the medium term.

It is, however, still possible to argue for a pricing reform which is consistent and feasible. A central concern of the subsidy system should be to ensure relative equality of subsidy at any given income level across all sectors. In setting prices based on market values in the social sector, it is essential to recognise that owner-occupiers do not make monthly payments based on current capital values, or even values indexed annually.

First, a fifth of owners purchased, often through Right to Buy, with very substantial discounts; (see chapter 5). Second, under British tax arrangements, all owners generally benefit from the passage of time. Even without inflation residents benefit from the non-taxation of 'imputed' rents. With inflation, the value of debt incurred at the date of purchase falls and there may be real capital gains; (again, see chapter 5).

The outcome of the payment system in owner-occupation is that, while purchasers in the current year make payments related to current capital values, non-moving owners do not. If the average owner moves every eleven years, then only a tenth of owners pay current prices and a tenth benefit from a decade of historic pricing. Whilst the 'historic-cost' component of payments changes over time for individual owners and falls to zero when they move, the sector as a whole will have a stable historic component if house-price inflation rates remain constant. Only if house-price inflation is zero will the historic-cost effect disappear.

The ratio of initial purchase-prices to current values of owner-occupied properties is shown in **Table 17**. Ratios are presented for the 'full-market values' and 'bottom-half values'. The latter figures suggest that, in five of the six markets, there is a 33 per cent

'discount' on market values for owners, and 43 per cent in London.

One means of ensuring that tenants have their dwellings priced comparably with owners is to reduce capital values in the council sector by a proportion comparable to the owned sector. This proportion is labelled 'historic weighting'.

Rents were re-estimated allowing no capital gains but with a 'historic-weighting' factor based upon the ratios in **Table 17**. The results, by region, are presented in **Table 18**.

With a 5.5 per cent rate of return, substantial rent increases, in the range of 40 to 100 per cent are

Table 17
Ratio of purchase price/current values

	Lower values	(All) market values
Bristol	0.683	0.696
Birmingham	0.674	0.500
Glasgow	0.691	0.523
London	0.567	0.560
Newcastle	0.682	0.582
Sheffield	0.692	0.230

Table 18

Estimated rent levels with 'historic weighting' but no capital gains

				Rents based on 'full-market values'		Rents based on bottom-half values	
		5.5% return		4% return		4% return	
	Current Gross Rent	With historic weighting	HW and 10pc fall	With historic weighting	HW and 10pc fall	With historic weighting	HW and 10pc fall
Birmingham	**1011**	**1353**	**1217**	**1130**	**1060**	**1254**	**911**
Bristol	**969**	**1412**	**1271**	**1184**	**1108**	**1084**	**1006**
Glasgow	**829**	**1232**	**1130**	**1045**	**986**	**1355**	**1220**
London	**1176**	**2649**	**2337**	**2630**	**2409**	**2292**	**1306**
Newcastle	**1046**	**948**	**853**	**827**	**788**	**1193**	**1073**
Sheffield	**1037**	**875**	**787**	**770**	**735**	**1193**	**1073**

implied, except in Newcastle and Sheffield where they would fall. A 4 per cent return on full-market values would also induce gross rent decreases in these two northern regions, increases of 10 to 20 per cent in other regions and a doubling in London.

Rents based upon 'bottom-half values' provide an even more feasible starting point for reform, particularly as they produce lower rents in London and Bristol. As this method of valuation has a principled rationale, it represents the best basis on which to proceed further, although our scepticism regarding the estimated values for London, for both 'full-market values' (too high) and 'bottom-half values' (too low) should be noted.

The effect of a fall in market values of 10 per cent is also shown in **Table 18.** to illustrate the argument that tenants benefit from restrained house prices; and lower prices would facilitate consistent pricing in the council sector and reduce housing benefit bills.

Pricing reform

The rent levels reported in the penultimate column of **Table 18** indicate a possible path to a reform of rent-setting and subsidy determination for council housing.

49

'Ring-fencing' chaos?

The overall rent increases are modest, and may already have been attained in real terms - London excepted - since the introduction of 'ring-fencing' in England; (this cannot be confirmed as 'bottom-half values' for 1991 are not available). The implication of the pricing scheme for housing benefit, simulated in Appendix 2, is that total bills would increase by 7 per cent.

The major advantage of the proposal is that the rents of dwellings would be set consistently across local authorities and for each property within each region. The latter aspect, which is crucial in an efficient use of council stock and distribution of housing benefit, is not part of the present 'ring-fencing' regime.

The proposal, like any other based upon capital values with a uniform national rate of return, has a number of possible weaknesses. What is being proposed is a national pricing scheme. Local authorities are unlikely to welcome such an approach. However, a two-part pricing system could assuage such criticism and encourage efficiency in the provision of management and maintenance services. Capital values should form the basis of only the property component of rent. Local authorities should be free to choose the levels of services provided and their costs. Two-part bills would make this split apparent to tenants. Rent Officers,

seeking to ensure value for money in the use of housing benefit, would be free to concentrate upon the costs and effectiveness of service delivery.

The new scheme, at current levels of the 'historic-weighting factor' implies a real rate of return close to 2.75 per cent, and 2.5 per cent in London. This means that producer subsidies will be required for new investment. Such subsidies are inevitable if government wishes to house low-income tenants at a standard of housing which they will not, usually cannot, pay for and at the same time seeks to retain a housing benefit system similar in structure and generosity to the present one.

If the pricing approach proposed were to be applied also to housing associations, as discussed in the next chapter, there would also be a case for making capital subsidies neutral across the social sectors. The nature of housing associations tends to suggest that such assistance should be in the form of a capital grant; and grant arrangements could be more neutral across all of the rented sector (assuming consistent pricing).

Should inflation occur in the future, councils will generate surpluses on their property holdings as rents are annually, automatically raised in line with capital values. These surpluses, as at present, could fund capital spending or contribute to housing benefit. However, surpluses generated in service provision, as long as Rent Officers judged they arose from efficiency gains and not unfair service rents, should be used at the discretion of the local authority, as they arise from effort rather than chance.

Conclusion

The present system of pricing council housing is unfair across authorities and inefficient within them. The pricing reform suggested would reduce such inconsistences and inefficiencies and promote a more effective use of housing benefit. Details exist, in databases of house prices across the country, which could make the system possible. Two-part rent bills and tenure-neutral capital grants would encourage local authorities to manage effectively and give them a role in future investment where they were the most efficient developers.

The independent rented sector

Light and shade

There is little in common between the images of the two components of the 'independent rented sector'. Housing associations have an image of being enlightened, 'not-for-profit' landlords, and a reputation for high standards of design, management and maintenance. They have been subsidised with large capital grants to provide housing for people who increasingly resemble those in the council sector.

In contrast, private rental housing in Britain has a poor reputation. It is explicitly 'for profit' and has historically been associated with low quality, badly maintained housing for older, poorer households. *Paying for Britain's Housing* outlined the diverse roles of the private rented sector; at the end of the 1980s there appeared to be at least a dual sector, not all of which was poor quality or inherently unsatisfactory for renters.

Taken together, the two segments of the sector house less than one household in ten in Britain. Both may grow in the 1990s.

False Dawn

The 1988 Housing Act gave associations an opportunity to play a major role in the expansion of the 'independent rented sector', and to counterbalance local authorities in the provision of social housing. The introduction of Tenants' Choice and a new impetus for local authority voluntary stock transfers indicated that, for future investment, associations were to be regarded as the 'second arm' of British housing policy.

These changes, and the associated deregulation of new lettings, raised expectations of expansion in the independent rented sector and predictions of the demise of council housing.

But it now appears as if the rental sector has more room than expected for local authorities and less room for the private rented sector. At current rates of investment and stock transfer, it is difficult to conceive of housing association stock being larger than that of local authorities by the year 2000. Competition from the profit-making private rented sector is limited by present subsidy and tax arrangements (aside from the BES incentives) and a large-scale revival of private provision is unlikely. False expectations, operational ambiguities ('output', 'efficiency', 'affordability') and a poorly designed housing finance policy have all contributed to the slow progress towards a diverse but expanding rental sector.

The changing role of housing associations

In March 1990, housing associations owned just 2.8 per cent of the nation's housing stock. While there are around 2,600 housing associations and co-operatives registered in Great Britain, three-quarters of the stock was was owned by the 5 per cent of associations with more than 1,000 units. Mergers induced by the new financial regime and the new, larger associations created to take over local authority stock, could change this profile significantly.

Contrary to common belief, there has not been constant growth in the size of the association sector in the 1980s. Although there was a shift in the balance of government capital spending in favour of the housing association programme, the overall real reduction in capital expenditure on housing meant that the resources allocated to housing associations did not rise significantly. **Figure 3** shows that real capital investment dipped between 1985 and 1988; and over the six year period to 1989/90 gross capital allocations rose by

Figure 3

Housing association programme, real expenditure 1984/85 to 1990/91

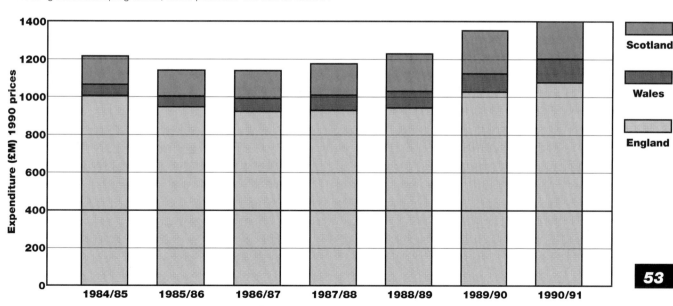

just 12 per cent in real terms. This pattern was most marked in England, where the Housing Corporation's budget rose by only 3 per cent over the period; but Scottish and Welsh housing associations fared much better, with real increases of 56 and 59 per cent respectively.

New housing approvals and completions funded by Housing Association Grant (HAG) in Great Britain averaged over 25,000 rented units between 1980 and 1990, but the rate slowed in the second half of the decade to around four-fifths of the previous five-year total. In 1989, the year before the introduction of the new financial regime, rental completions from the housing association programme fell to its lowest level since 1976/77.

Although sometimes erratic, associations' growth was nevertheless significant. Kleinman (1) notes that in England and Wales, associations expanded their stock by almost 50 per cent between 1981 and 1987. However, expansion was from a small base and uneven across the country. Growth was most marked in Wales (+114 per cent), the Midlands (+64 per cent), the North-West (+87per cent) and Yorkshire (+37 per cent) and lowest in London (+37 per cent) and the South-East (+19 per cent). Apart from London, the programme favoured the conurbations and large cities (+65 per cent) rather than rural areas (+28 per cent). Since 1986-87, changes in regional allocations have re-favoured the South and rural areas.

Resource distribution has also been influenced by the pattern of regional construction costs. Higher unit costs in London and the South-East have resulted in allocations which, by the Corporation's own admission, were skewed away from these pressurised areas (2). The Housing Corporation, and its Scottish and Welsh counterparts, have also tended to concentrate resources in 'stress' areas, on the grounds that this maximised the benefit obtained from relatively scarce resources (3). The important value of such 'spillover' benefits from the association programme may not have been adequately addressed by the new financial regime.

Capital allocations have not been made strictly in accordance with housing 'need' as measured by the Housing Needs Indicator (HNI). A report for the Association of District Councils (4) raised concerns that the North had received a disproportionate share of resources. The revised HNI now includes an indicator which attempts to draw a distinction between need and demand; this change should favour the South, but at the same time increase the 'regional policy' effects of housing policy favouring such areas.

The Housing Corporation's budget for the years 1991/92 to 1993/94 is now set to increase significantly, rising from an estimated out-turn of £1.1 billion in 1990/91 to £1.8 billion in 1993/94. Funds raised from the private sector will add to these totals. In consequence, output from the (English) programme is expected to rise to 40,000 units in the year to 31 March, 1994. Over four-fifths of these are planned to be rented units. The housing association movement will also grow through the voluntary transfer programme, which to date has been entirely funded by bank or building society borrowing and thus additional to the expenditure levels set out above. (In Scotland where the local authority sector still dominates the rental sector and the private rental sector is small, Scottish Homes appears to face little prospect of such a major expansion.)

Who lives in housing association homes?

After the introduction of Housing Association Grant in 1974, associations provided housing for low income groups. Early programmes concentrated on the provision of rented housing. Rehabilitation accounted for a sizeable proportion of the programme, though

levels have fallen throughout the 1980s and have continued to do so since the introduction of the new financial regime. It is only in Scotland that association-led rehabilitation has been a major instrument of urban regeneration policy. Provision of 'special needs' accommodation - for the elderly, disabled and single people - has also been a priority, although there has been increasing investment in low-cost home ownership, introduced in 1980, which now accounts for 10 per cent of the programme. Recent special initiatives for the homeless add to what is now a more diverse programme.

A number of surveys (5) have been carried out into the circumstances of housing association tenants. The predominant group housed by associations are single adults: including the single elderly, this group formed between 51 per cent (England) and 70 per cent (Scotland) of all new lettings. Elderly households accounted for around one third of the total.

Less than a third of heads of household were in full- or part-time work, around one third were retired and one fifth were unemployed.

Incomes were low. Net weekly income across all households was less than £100 per week with the majority group of single-person households among the lowest. Households with no-one in work had net incomes of around £60 per week, about half the income level of those with at least one member working. Not surprisingly, over 50 per cent of households were dependent on housing benefit to meet their housing costs.

In *Paying for Britain's Housing*, we questioned undue reliance on simple rent-to-income or 'affordability' ratios as an indicator of the ability of households to pay for adequate housing. The National Federation's affordability ratio expresses average rent as a proportion of median net income for households with at least one working member. For the fourth quarter of 1990, the actual ratio stood at 22.8 per cent compared with the Federation's 20 per cent 'guideline'. The Welsh Federation found the ratio in the first quarter of 1990/91 to be 23 per cent, and the Scottish survey noted that those households where the household head was in full employment spent an average of 17 per cent on rent. The Foundation's survey revealed an average net expenditure (after deducting housing benefit) to income ratio of 17 per cent for all households.

Subsidies for housing association tenants

Housing association tenants are subsidised in a different fashion from council tenants. Before the new financial regime, 'fair' rents were set by rent officers. After making an allowance for management and maintenance costs, net proceeds from rents would then be used to support a 'residual loan'. The gap between approved project costs (sanctioned by the Housing Corporation) and the residual loan was closed by a payment of HAG. Recurrent subsidies, in the form of Revenue Deficit Grant, were small in scale and designed to cope with unexpected levels of management and maintenance costs. HAG levels commonly ran up to and over 80 per cent of project costs.

Results from the Foundation's survey (6) indicated that property characteristics explained, on average, 35 per cent of the observed variation in fair rents for each region (7). Association rents were more consistently related to property quality than in the council sector and this reflects the effect of Rent Officer pricing. Since associations now have no clear, central guidance in rent-setting – a critical area of policy 'ambiguity' – the relative strength of this relationship will not necessarily have been maintained.

Actual gross rents, which were relatively uniform across the regions, but with London significantly higher and Glasgow markedly lower, are indicated in **Table 19**.

This Table also sets out estimated market rents using different assumptions about rates of return, capital gains and property values. If expected gains in house prices are zero and rates of return at 5.5 per cent are required (to attract private finance), the prospect is daunting for associations; based on 1989 values, rents would have had to rise by 80 to 125 per cent across the regions. However, if local capital gains contribute to a real return of 4 per cent at their historic rates on lower 'market values' (the criterion used in chapter 3), rent increases are only likely to be problematic in Birmingham (40 per cent) and particularly Glasgow (90 per cent).

Estimates of subsidies are set out in **Table 20** and are based on a 4 per cent rate of return, including local capital gain applied to estimated capital values for the bottom half of the market. The difference between estimated market rents and gross rents indicates that in the areas of higher capital gain, actual gross rents were closer to imputed market rents. In Glasgow, where actual rents and capital gain rates were low, estimated market rents were double those prevailing. Subsidy based on comparison with net rents reflects the additional cash subsidy arising through the housing benefit system. Again, it is greatest in areas of least house-price appreciation.

Table 19

Gross rents, net rents and ranges of market rents for the housing association sector

			No capital gain		Capital gain deducted	
	Actual	*Actual*	*Full market*	*Bottom*	*Local gain rates*	
	gross rent	*net rent*	*value (5.5)*	*half (4.0)*	*Full market (5.5)*	*Bottom half (4.0)*
Birmingham	1045	783	2481	1859	1954	1448
Bristol	1073	668	2547	1995	1401	1099
Glasgow	828	608	2657	1870	2278	1593
London	1160	892	5252	2231	2566	1171
Newcastle	1078	603	1572	1697	1171	1208
Sheffield	1050	716	1731	1741	1108	1068

The independent rented sector

When association subsidies were compared with council subsidies in each region, the average subsidy per association tenant was lower in five of the six areas, with the exception of Glasgow. In most regions, the distortion of rent levels was a less important source of subsidy for association than for council tenants and, as in the council sector, housing benefit was the main form of support.

In the market-value measure of subsidies, HAG levels are irrelevant as rents were set independently under the fair rent system. However, HAG expenditures are relevant in a comparison of HAG expenditure per unit in relation to the values of dwellings in the lower half of the current housing market. In most of the case

studies, HAG per house exceeds estimated market value by between 15 and 20 per cent. This merely reaffirms the point made in chapter 3: the lower end of the market would never effectively demand the size or quality of units provided by associations.

The HAG-value gap reflects some 'social' valuation placed upon the assumed benefit of housing the poor in better homes, or a valuation of the benefits which good housing provides to adjacent and other residents, especially in rehabilitation areas. As part of the programme, an estimate was made of the value of these spillover benefits in housing rehabilitation by associations in Glasgow (8). It was estimated that such benefits could reach half the value of HAG per house.

Table 20

Annual subsidy estimates for housing association tenants (based on 4.0% return, bottom-half values, local capital gain deducted)

	Gross rent	Net rent	Estimated market rent	Gross rent subsidy	Estmated subsidy	Mean HB payment	Subsidies / market rent (%)
Birmingham	1045	783	1448	403	665	262	46
Bristol	1073	668	1099	36	431	405	39
Glasgow	828	608	1593	767	985	220	62
London	1160	892	1171	17	279	268	24
Newcastle	1078	603	1208	142	605	475	50
Sheffield	1050	716	1068	24	353	329	33

If the same outcomes had been sought without HAG and with market rents and housing benefit, the public expenditure costs would have been greater. And residents would have been in a cavernous poverty trap, paying for a housing standard they did not 'demand'. Producer subsidies are an efficient approach in such circumstances.

For all housing association households in the survey, **Table 21** shows the patterns of rents and subsidies by income group, ethnic status, distance from the city centre and age of dwelling. A number of interesting observations emerge. Gross rents do not show a progressive relationship with income, but the fair rent system explicitly excluded any account of household circumstances. Estimated market rents, on the other hand, rise with income, suggesting that better-off households occupy higher valued property. This may be a function of household and property size.

These patterns imply that, within the association sector, the least well-off households enjoy the least rent subsidy. The gap between estimated market-value rents and gross rents falls in line with increasing distance from city centres. Subsidies are closer to city centres and for older (rehabilitated) homes. Although the small sample size prevents a robust conclusion, the

result indicates that 'white' and 'non-white' households in association homes received similar benefits from rent distortions and this contrasts with the council sector (see chapter 3).

Between the first quarter of 1989 and the third quarter of 1990, the NFHA's all-rent index shows a rise in association rents of 25 per cent. This implies a real rent increase of close to 11 per cent over the period and a significant reduction in the gap between estimated market value and actual gross rents, which would be in the order of 20 per cent.

This gap will have narrowed further where real property values have declined since 1989; but data is unavailable for the specific segment of the housing market in which the associations operate. If average regional price shifts applied to such areas, then the combination of real rent increases and capital value reductions would have further reduced subsidies from pricing in southern Britain.

Consistent pricing across the main tenures has been a theme of this report. Chapter 3 questioned the assumption that real capital gains will contribute to required returns as they did in the 1980s; and it was shown that a 'historic weighting factor' was required

The independent rented sector

Table 21
Estimates of subsidies in the housing association sector (based on 4% return, bottom-half values, local capital gain)

	Estimated market value		Gross rent	Net rent	Market value divided by gross rent	Rent 'distortion' subsidy	Housing Benefit
Income group							
< 2600	1250	(45)	1058	409	1.18	192	649
2600-5199	1327	(62)	1039	553	1.28	289	486
5200-7199	1316	(21)	910	730	1.45	406	180
> 7800	1385	(122)	1124	1015	1.23	261	109
Ethnic status							
White	1304	(217)	1042	726	1.25	262	284
Non-White	1275	(33)	1062	655	1.21	213	407
Distance from city centre (km)							
< 5	1321	(154)	998	652	1.32	323	346
5.01-10	1281	(78)	1091	802	1.17	190	289
10.01-15	1211	(11)	1070	695	1.13	141	375
> 15	1231	(10)	1161	1107	1.06	70	54
Age of building							
Pre-1919	1304	(73)	907	647	1.43	403	260
1919-44	1303	(57)	920	649	1.42	383	271
Post 1944	1288	(117)	1179	784	1.09	109	395

to ensure comparable pricing for owners and renters in the social sector.

A 'historic-weighted, no-capital-gains' estimate was produced for the association properties in the regions.

Such a scheme would, using 1989 values, have implied marginal rent increases or decreases in five of the six regions, with only Glasgow's rents rising significantly if a 4 per cent return was to be realised incorporating the 'historic weighting factor'. However, if in 1989 associations had been faced with raising a 5.5 per cent rate of return and no prospect of capital gain, then rents would have risen by 60 per cent. In the absence of the 'weighting' factor, the increase would have been in excess of 100 per cent.

Reforming the new regime?

The possible pricing reform suggested for the council sector set out in chapter 3 is broadly compatible with the current 'ring-fencing' approach; and it may reinforce efficiency through consistent local pricing. However, the principle of a two-part rent scheme with the property component fixed in relation to local market values (appropriately weighted) is more difficult to reconcile with the post-1989 regime for associations.

The objectives of this regime are the promotion of 'value for money' in development and management and the expansion of private finance in the sector. These were the key reforms:

- HAG should cease to be an open-ended commitment; rates were to be pre-determined and associations (in reality their tenants or the housing benefit system) were to bear the costs where out-turn expenditures exceeded forecasts;

- Fair rents, in consequence, were abandoned for new lettings; associations were to set 'affordable' rents.

- Revenue Deficit Grant was to be scrapped, as it rewarded management inefficiency and also effectively represented a Treasury guarantee for private funds;

- the Grant Redemption Fund (instituted after 1980 to recapture inflation gains from associations) was transformed into the Rent Surplus Fund. These surpluses are generally earmarked for major repairs though 15 per cent is returned to the Housing Corporation;

- residual loans, financed from the private sector, were no longer to be regarded as 'public', thus allowing an expansion of programmes from any given level of public funding;

- rents should include an allowance to pay for future, major repairs;

The system has operated a little differently in Scotland but the broad principles are similar, though HAG rates are not pre-determined.

The two-part, rent-setting proposal would not disturb or displace all of these changes:

- it would encourage the effective provision of services, chosen locally, no less than the present regime; and it would not require the re-introduction of RDG or an equivalent;

- it would ensure provision for future, major repairs; the rent-setting exercise makes allowance for depreciation;

- it would require a Rent Surplus Fund having separate property and service components. The latter, arising from management efficiencies of associations, would be kept in its entirety. The formal allowance system for management and maintenance spending could be scrapped, though local rent officers would require guidance on assessing service provision costs;

- surpluses on the property account, arising from windfall gains in property values, could be shared on the basis of the ratio of HAG to private finance in specific projects. This would also provide associations with an incentive to economise initially on the use of HAG.

The major point of departure arises in relation to the requirement to set the property component of rents on a predetermined, national rent-setting basis. This would imply that HAG and not rent was the 'residual' in the system. Government may be unwilling to relax its belief that real efficiency gains arise from pre-fixing HAG rates and/or levels.

However, such gains may also arise from reductions in standards, shifts in programme mix and location and from rent increases, which do not indicate increased association efficiency or effectiveness. Evidence is beginning to highlight some early trends. Research in Scotland (8) demonstrated that public funds had been 'stretched' by almost 40 per cent over a nine-month period; but that one third of the increase was attributable to the transfer of residual loans to the private sector, a further 15 per cent to a real reduction in unit costs and the remaining 50 per cent to a combination of rising real rents and lower revenue costs.

No comparable evidence was available from England or Wales but if the patterns are similar then the efficiency gains, defined as savings in real resources, have been modest. In a world of scarce resources it is possible that similar gains could have been made by the supervisory bodies considering past overspending by an association (at least relative to regional averages) in making annual cash allocations.

Rent increases have clearly outweighed efficiency gains in adapting to the new regime. But is this process fair when it passes on unexpected costs to low-income tenants? And is this efficient if it raises housing benefit bills?

The capital-value-based rent-setting scheme proposed here would free associations from setting the property component of rents. Rent levels distorted to meet local incomes and rent-pooling are two features of the council housing system which critics, including government, have regarded unfavourably in the past. They do not make any more sense in the housing association sector. The proposed system would pitch rents at approximately their present levels, implying minimal changes in the overall levels of housing benefit, and would have an estimated rent-to-income ratio of just over 20 per cent. The implied rate of return on capital values would be 2.75 per cent, but of course the presence of HAG (at prevailing levels) would ensure private finance returns at present levels.

The small scale of the association sample in the survey and the absence of comparable data for 1991 means that these proposals would need to be re-tested before they formed the basis for policy change. But the desirability of a uniform, tenure-neutral pricing system for social housing does require that these issues be confronted and not sunk in a froth of ambiguous slogans.

Experience with private finance

The commitment of private funds for investment by associations has already been considerable (see **Table 22**) but such success has been neither uniform nor cheap. Experience to date suggests that difficulty in raising private finance is greatest for small associations. Research suggested that lenders tended to 'discriminate against smaller, less well-established associations without a clear track record' (9). A survey carried out in Scotland to assess the initial impact of the new financial regime 10) found that, while four out of five associations had encountered no difficulty in raising private funds, those which had problems tended to be small, often housing co-operatives. Many of these small organisations are integral to regeneration policies.

In seeking to minimise the risk of borrowing failures, the Housing Corporation has developed criteria by which it assesses the capacity of associations to use private funds; they are based on measures of property equity and free reserves. The Corporation and Scottish Homes have also made strenuous efforts to seek out funding sources, engaging in discussion with lenders and training with associations. Research has confirmed slow progress up the learning curve (11); although the position is continuing to improve, considerable uncertainty remains. The City may have developed a jaundiced view of 'public' investment in the wake of the local authority, interest-rate-swap debacle and the problems of financial control at the Housing Corporation.

Lenders are uncertain about the public-private, hybrid nature of housing associations as well as the unappetising appearance of association balance sheets; this is not only reflected in a bias towards larger, more financially secure associations, but in the 'risk premiums' attached to their lending terms. Margins over base rates, often in the range of 1 to 3 per cent, compare unfavourably with government borrowing terms. The Building Society Commission's prescribed capital adequacy ratios require lending to housing associations for rented housing to be backed by greater provisions - similar reserve weightings are applied by the Bank of England - than for lending to home-owners, thus increasing the cost of funds. It is likely that some losses made in lending to unregistered housing associations, largely on ventures for sale, may be responsible for this. Couttie believes that whilst

experience demonstrates lending for rented housing to be less risky, investors' "perceptions can carry more weight than the facts".

These issues emphasise the need for continued dialogue to increase further mutual understanding between associations and lenders, but they also underline the importance of registration with the Housing Corporation whose encouragement of prudential management, scheme scrutiny and monitoring procedures can offer lenders a form of 'comfort'.

Of equal importance is the level of security provided to lenders by HAG, illustrated in the Scottish context, where the housing association programme has so far been funded at an approximate average grant rate of 85 per cent, and long-term borrowing margins average 0.25%.

A second and related concern is the supply of finance which, if restricted, will also increase borrowing costs. At the outset of the new financial regime, the new but unknown market for housing association lending created a surge of interest, but this has since narrowed. Many lenders decided that more secure investments could be made elsewhere without time spent on the learning curve. Alternative investments such as gilts

Table 22

Estimated private funding requirements, 1989-1993 (£m)

	1989/90	1990/91	1991/92	1992/93
England:				
Vol Transfers	125	715	400*	400*
Mixed Funding	175	225	387	463
100% private†	175	225	387	463
Scotland+	7	35	55	n/a
Wales	25	33	37	40
Total	507	1233	1262	1366

Notes:

* Estimates from Couttie (1991)

† HC estimates 100% private will match mixed funding

+ Requirement for Scottish Homes' 'Enabling' programme

Sources:

Housing Corporation Private Finance Section, Scottish Homes Second Strategic Plan, Tai Cymru

and equities remain in strong competition. Couttie points to the wave of recent government privatisations as an example, with social housing not amongst the key attractions.

Most lending for mixed-funded projects has been by building societies and banks, with the latter dominant in transfers of local authority stock (using no public funding) which, although small in number, have involved the transfer, to March 1991, of 75,000 homes and have consumed the lion's share of private funds.

Many lenders, particularly banks and, contrary to expectations, insurance companies and pension funds, prefer shorter-term lending. Although pension funds and insurance companies have long-term liabilities, they heavily discount future capital gains and are fearful of exposure to inflation. Improved appraisal of equity options has increased their involvement in equity markets and they have no real tradition of holding corporate debt. Index-linked loans are still probably their preferred funding route. If the estimated requirements for private funding - around £1.3 billion for the current year (**Table 22**) - are to be met, there is clearly a need to develop funding mechanisms which match lenders' and borrowers' requirements more closely.

The early mixed-funded initiatives were financed by index-linked loans pioneered by the Nationwide Anglia and Halifax Building Societies. As index-linked funds became more scarce, deferred interest loans became more common. In addition, a variety of other low-start loan instruments have been used, including zero-coupon bonds and stepped-interest loans provided through The Housing Finance Corporation (THFC).

Many associations and most participating lenders probably have a preference for conventional financing mechanisms rather than the low-start form expected in the new financial regime. To assume that associations would put all their eggs into one basket was ill-considered , especially since private-sector firms would be unlikely to adopt such a strategy. As well as presenting a riskier option, low-start finance is usually more expensive, total repayments are higher, and yields a low initial cash flow to lenders. But where grant is low there has been a greater need to borrow on low-start terms in order to keep rents affordable. Various equity-based models are being considered as an alternative but these have drawbacks in rented housing. First, the limited ability of investors to realise their asset value easily; second, the increasing belief that property will not experience the same levels of real gain achieved over the last two decades.

Low-start and fixed interest funds present a particular difficulty for long-term funding because they are not liquid and are based on assumptions about what the distant future will hold. Michael Pryke believes a true test of the market's interest in long-term funding of social housing will come about when development funds taken out in 1987/88 come up for re-financing (12).

Meanwhile, Couttie concludes that some form of guarantee or 'credit enhancement' may be required if the costs of private borrowing for housing associations are to be reduced and a steady supply of funds maintained. We believe that the development of a secondary mortgage market would facilitate the issue of long-term debt, whilst permitting investors the desired flexibility and liquidity. A well-capitalised THFC, which presently has no real capital base, or similar organisation could retail mortgage-backed securities, transforming risk over a large and growing pool of loans which could also form a focus for the high-street 'share shops' which the Chancellor now intends to promote.

The private rented sector

In *Paying for Britain's Housing*, it was noted that in the six case studies the private rented sector housed different groups and that their mix varied from region to region. In the North, around half the sample were older, often poor, households who lived in small, inner city, poor-quality pre-1919 properties. In all regions, there was a minority of younger, usually single, poor households in this sector. And in the southern conurbations of Bristol and London, the largest group was small, middle- and above-average-income households residing in adequate housing with unregistered rents.

With at least half of the sector already effectively in a market regime, the rent decontrol of 1989 was likely to have moderate impacts. The local case study teams confirmed that the unregistered rent sector, often associated with furnished lets, had been relatively stable in size in the 1980s, with some modest expansion in some locations, for instance Bristol. Landlords were estimated to be earning total real returns of 6-8 per cent.

In the registered sector, vacant possession usually resulted in properties being switched to less regulated forms of tenancy or in properties being sold into owner-occupation. This pattern is consistent with other studies. Registered sector accommodation rents were set by Rent Officers at below-market levels before 1989, with potential surpluses for landlords being translated into lower rents for tenants. Rents in such properties could also be defrayed by housing benefit payments. In the non-registered sector, housing benefit was available to qualifying tenants; around a quarter of tenants received it in 1989.

The tax and subsidy position of private landlords was radically different from owner-occupation and social housing. Unlike home-owners, landlords are taxed on the income from their properties and on the realised capital gains from selling properties; and unlike the social rental sector, private landlords receive no recurrent subsidies; capital grants were available to

The independent rented sector

them only for home improvement in the 1980s, and at a less generous rate than in the other sectors.

Subsidies to private tenants

The broad pattern of subsidies, defined as the gap between estimated market rents and rents paid, is indicated in **Table 23**. In order to make the estimates comparable with previous results, market-value rents are based on the assumption that real total rates of return are 4 per cent on the 'bottom half' of the

market values of property; and they are earned after deducting similar management and maintenance allowances as for the social sector.

Three of these assumptions may be questionable. First, it can be argued that investment in private rental housing is riskier (not least politically) than the social sector. A higher 'allowed' rate of return would generate larger estimates of subsidy values. Second, some properties in the unregulated sector lie above the

Table 23

Subsidies in the private rental sectors (4.0% return, bottom-half values minus local capital gain)

	Registered rents			Unregistered rents		
	Rent subsidies	HB	All subsidies	Rent subsidies	HB	All subsidies
<2,600	197	472	869	350	222	572
2,600-5,199	321	346	667	189	344	533
5,200-7,799	18	198	216	-73	231	158
7,800-10,399	245	51	296	-134	256	122
10,400-12,999	156	10	166	-639	160	-479
Birmingham	596	186	782	413	103	516
Bristol	-22	404	382	0	124	124
Glasgow	743	276	1019	438	118	556
London	-200	124	-76	-562	115	-447
Newcastle	238	219	557	191	231	422
Sheffield	224	94	418	76	35	111

regional average value and should be weighted by different price factors. It is assumed that this latter effect is not important. Third, it is also recognised that controlled rents may result in reductions in service quality which diminish the effective subsidy received by households; (this observation applies to other tenures). This study cannot estimate this effect and, in consequence, probably over-values subsidies to tenants.

The subsidy patterns estimated for private tenants have a number of important features. In the 'registered' rent sector, rent distortions (transferring resources from landlords to tenants) are on a greater per capita scale than in the social rented sector. This observation does not apply, however, in Bristol and London, where the registered sector is not only relatively smaller than the un-registered market but also has closer pricing affinities with the market sector. Indeed, in these two areas registered rents support gross returns in excess of 4 per cent. Housing benefit has a variable role in the registered sector in delivering overall subsidies to tenants, being most important in Bristol, Glasgow and Newcastle.

In the un-registered sector, tenants in Bristol received no rent distortion subsidies and in London paid rents well above a 4 per cent return level, even where they were supported by housing benefit. In the other regions, there was still a significant gap between actual gross rents and estimated market values, although it was lower than rent distortion subsidies in the social sector. Either landlords earn less than 4 per cent in such areas, which is not consistent with the 6 to 8 per cent returns noted by some case study teams, or their management and maintenance costs and depreciation allowance fall well below our assumed levels.

The value of rent distortion subsidies in the registered sector shows no clear relationship to household income. However, it is clearly related to property and resident age and location. Households over 60 years old received an average 'distortion' in their favour of £329 per annum, 45- 60 year olds £190, and younger households less than £100. Long-term, usually older and poor residents, received the largest subsidies and often in central city locations (subject to the caveat about quality already noted). Clearly such arrangements favour immobility.

In the unregistered sector, subsidies fell progressively with income levels, though this result may reflect quality variation and 'market segment' effects not allowed for in the valuation procedures.

Changes after 1988

No sooner had these patterns been observed than the legislative framework changed. After 1989, landlords were generally free to set market rents on new lettings across the sector as a whole, though this change will not yet have made an impact on continuing, registered tenancies. In 1988, the government extended the Business Expansion Scheme to encourage new investment in rental housing, thus allowing major tax concessions to this form of rental housing. BES investors can secure income tax relief on investment up to a limit of £40,000 of capital and are exempted from capital gains tax when disposing of assets after five years.

These changes have diversified the sector. A recent study reports that from 1988 to 1990, 188 rental housing companies raised £461 million, and let 8,200 homes, 5,400 newly built **(13)**. The foregone tax revenues are likely to be of the order of £225 million, thus providing a tax subsidy of around half cost of the dwellings (which had an average unit price of £54,000).

These subsidies were reinforced by housing benefit as a fifth of tenants had received or had applied for assistance. The majority of tenants were, however, young adults in non-manual jobs and rents of £67 per week on average, ranged from £49 in the North to £99 in London. The average income level of recipients (tenant and partner) of BES properties was £14,606. This reform, in effect, stimulated investment by providing subsidies to middle- and upper-income renters.

A very different view of post-1988 change in the private rental sector emerges from a study by SHAC of the experience of private sector tenants in London seeking help from housing advice agencies **(14)**. In that sample, less than half of those surveyed had jobs, the majority were not white, and two-fifths received housing benefit. A quarter reported being harassed and a third claimed poor dwelling conditions or overcrowding. A quarter had or were about to apply to the local authority for housing on the grounds on homelessness.

One reform or two?

These studies illustrate the diversity within British private rental housing. One broad policy framework is expected to operate effectively for quite different groups: BES tenants, many of them no doubt heading on to owner-occupation, have benefited from the broad policy thrust; the SHAC sample had either been left untouched or had their experiences exacerbated by policy change.

In our view it is impossible to develop a coherent, all-embracing policy for subsidising private rental housing. Low-income groups in private tenancies compare with the social sectors in relation to needs and resources. Higher-income groups have home-ownership incomes and aspirations. The goals of meeting need and facilitating housing and labour market mobility may be mutually contradictory.

Policy development can confront these divergences in a more effective fashion by recognising the diversity of the sector. Where private landlords meet the mobility demands of younger and other households on incomes which are above or near average, then the appropriate finance regime for landlords should be harmonised with home-owners.

If the present regime for owners were to be maintained, then the expansion of rental housing may require landlords to be allowed to set maintenance and depreciation costs against tax obligations on income from letting. Landlords, unlike owners, pay capital gains tax; some form of capital grant (or tax exemption) would be required to equalise fiscal privileges. Such tax concessions would at present imply an annual tax subsidy to landlords at a third of BES levels of £1,500 per let (assuming a total real return of 4 per cent per annum, and an average value house).

Such a shift in policy, implying a 'level playing-field' for private landlords, is unlikely to command Treasury or political support, even if it is a precondition for achieving government policy in this area. But, as a first step, it would not be impossible to allow landlords a depreciation allowance equal to the level of average mortgage interest tax relief, presently around £750 per annum, which may move downwards over time.

Private landlords and low income tenants

A tax-related policy reform of this nature would not be a suitable approach for landlords whose main aim was to continue letting to low income tenants. In this instance, the point of comparison is with councils and the housing association sector.

The 1989 reforms expected or hoped that private landlords would be able to compete with councils and associations for tenants seeking to transfer from landlords offering poor-quality accommodation. Even where 'new-style' landlords have managed to shake off the traditional image of the sector, the present financial regime largely precludes such competition. Landlords have relied upon purchasing discounted social sector properties, hidden land-cost subsidies and occasional capital grants, through Urban Development Grant in England and 'GRO-Grants' in Scotland (15), to make small inroads. Private, as distinct from social, landlords cannot be asked to accept 'historical' weightings on capital values, not least because they do pay capital gains tax.

The essential difficulty of the finance and subsidy regime is that it is not tenure neutral. The investment subsidies that a landlord receives do not depend solely upon the social or private purpose of a project – namely who is to be housed and with whatever wider benefits - but are also influenced by the legal status of the investor. This dilemma for policy can only be addressed by tenure-neutral, capital-value pricing, neutral-investment subsidies and equivalent rights for tenants. The present system precludes such an approach and it is also inhibited by our pricing proposals for social rented housing which have been 'historically weighted' to ensure fairness with owner-occupiers.

Where government or its agencies have a view that a particular area requires projects of a particular type for certain kinds of people, it should be in a position to tender the project to all potential investors, social and private, and accept the lowest bid for public resources. This would require project standards to be pre-determined; and that private landlords offered 'social tenancies', agreed to licensing and were subject to the same monitoring processes as housing associations. But unless private landlords were to be markedly more efficient than the social sector, consistent cross-tenure pricing of these essentially social projects would invariably imply higher grants to private landlords.

The range of powers of Scottish Homes, who provide HAG for associations and capital grants of up to 40 per cent of capital costs for private landlords through 'GRO-grants', means that this trade-off already exists in the allocation of funds. But it is made in a disorganised context of different rights and obligations. The real niche for subsidised private landlords may well be in providing for households who have incomes above the ranges typical of the social rented sector.

If the private rented sector is to play an enlightened, expanded role in British housing it has to be rethought and soon.

A redefined spectrum

Housing subsidies in the housing association sector are in general fairly distributed and well targeted. The new financial regime has introduced important innovations; but pricing in the sector may now be problematic and there is merit in reconsidering it, harmonising rents with a carefully priced council sector. Similarly, a tenure-neutral approach to capital funding in the social sector would underpin a genuine level playing-field for tenants and investors.

There are no clear ways in which private landlords catering for a disadvantaged clientele can harmonise pricing with social landlords, unless extensive capital grants or major new tax concessions are offered. It may serve the economy and the public purse better if limited tax concessions allowed landlords to compete more directly for the younger and mobile household whose long term aim is to become a home-owner.

The 1988 Housing Act intended enlightened structural reforms but the financial framework to promote with realism a diverse rental sector still needs to be fully developed.

Supporting home ownership

*Mortgage interest tax relief now reduces the UK tax revenue by £8 billion (see **Table 5**). The sums lost through the failure to tax capital gains on the sale of primary residences are also considerable (1). Home ownership is effectively untaxed (apart from Stamp Duty) and this means the home-owner (or mortgagor) receives significant subsidies in the form of such tax concessions.*

This chapter complements chapter 1 by examining the distribution of these tax expenditures. There is also an investigation of the financial benefits accruing to those former council tenants who purchased at discount through the Right to Buy; and a final section considers the role and incidence of property taxation.

We analyse three key tax expenditures: relief on mortgage interest payments; the imputed income tax liability; and the liability arising from capital gains tax. It must be made clear that not all constitute subsidies; but it is worth-while to discuss each one in the absence of consensus about how subsidies to owners should best be calculated (2).

Tax relief on mortgage interest payments acts as a cash-flow subsidy, whereas the absence of taxation of the benefits of occupation (from imputed income and from capital gains) relate to the underlying economic subsidies. It must be emphasised that the levels of subsidy discussed in this chapter are of cash magnitudes only and not the real value of extra housing actually received as a result of having the subsidy. Where housing supply responds sluggishly to price signals, subsidies could be self-defeating as they raise house prices (see chapter 1) (3)

The UK tax system is inconsistent across a number of dimensions. It can be considered a combination of two elements: the taxing of nominal and real income, depending on whether allowances are indexed to the rate of inflation (of which there is no in-built guarantee). It is inconsistent because, for historical and political reasons, marginal tax rates vary by taxable activity and with respect to the class of asset. For instance, corporate income is taxed more heavily than personal income. Such discrepancies lead to real economic distortions by attracting activity into the more lightly taxed areas and away from commodities taxed punitively.

Measures of subsidy must deal with these issues. No attempt is made here to design the discussion of subsidy around an ideal tax system, such as a comprehensive real income tax. Insofar as is possible, subsidy measures are based on the current tax system (with the exception of the imputed rental income tax).

Mortgage interest tax relief

Mortgagors are entitled to tax relief on the full value of their mortgage interest payments up to a mortgage ceiling of £30,000. Since 1983, the system has been greatly simplified by the Mortgage Interest Tax Relief At Source (MIRAS) scheme operated by building societies: the mortgage lender reduces interest payments on the assumption that the mortgagor is liable to the standard rate of income tax; the lender then claims the lost interest directly from the Inland Revenue. In this way, the subsidy operates as a simple reduction in the net mortgage rate faced by the borrower. Until the 1991 Budget, tax relief was available at the household's marginal tax rate: the top rate taxpayer had to claim the difference between his eligibility and MIRAS directly from the Inland Revenue.

The calculation here of mortgage interest tax relief follows the approach used by the case study teams, particularly that of Bristol (**4**). This entailed calculating outstanding mortgage debt and then applying the appropriate gross interest rate (averaged at 13.3% for the survey period) and the appropriate marginal tax rate

Table 24

Average mortgage interest tax relief

	Mean tax relief (£)	Cases
Total	513	1778
Birmingham	469	290
Bristol	566	406
Glasgow	558	172
London	625	336
Newcastle	450	313
Sheffield	392	261

(25 or 40 per cent). For those with endowment mortgages, outstanding debt is taken to be the entire mortgage (with tax relief on the first £30,000).

In **Table 24**, the average mortgage interest tax relief varied from less than £400 in Sheffield to over £600 in London, while the average for all cases is £513 per annum (over £100 less than the national average for that year). **Table 25** shows the unfair nature of the cash flow sub-sidy which rises with every band of income except for the bottom decile; households in the top income decile receive more than five times as much as those in the lowest decile. Owners had to to earn more than £20,799 per annum in order to receive the average subsidy.

Supporting home ownership

When the distribution of mortgage interest tax relief is disaggregated to the six case studies, with little exception, there is a strong positive link between gross banded income and the cash flow subsidy (**Table 26**). In London, apart from two extreme deciles, and Sheffield apart for the top decile, the pattern is broadly the same. In Bristol, London and Newcastle, the top decile of income receives around ten times the level of subsidy received by the bottom decile.

The distribution of mortgage interest tax relief by estimated property values is indicated in **Table 27**. MITR is fairly flat for the first four to five deciles (that is for house prices below £40,000) before the level of tax

Table 25

Mortgage interest tax relief by gross income band
£ per annum

Income band	Mean MITR	Number of cases
0-2,599	191.47	18
2,600-5,199	126.26	63
5,200-7,799	283.58	107
7,800-10,399	300.41	177
10,400-12,999	404.54	235
13,000-15,599	439.95	292
15,600-20,799	488.38	411
20,800-25,999	748.35	251
26,000-31,199	887.60	137
31,200 or more	1,001.78	82

Table 26

Mortgage interest tax relief by income band by area

Income band	Birmingham	Bristol	Glasgow	London	Newcastle	Sheffield
0-2,599	279	99	151	90	75	313
2,600-5,199	164	83	85	29	114	143
5,200-7,799	235	266	285	468	284	230
7,800-10,399	260	364	364	346	252	289
10,400-12,999	344	435	445	552	361	367
13,000-15,599	390	491	473	504	416	355
15,600-20,799	505	565	545	421	456	388
20,800-25,999	786	708	849	852	696	606
26,000-31,199	1,077	873	968	848	912	767
31,200 or more	1,203	1,182	971	1,015	1,003	452

Table 27

Mortgage interest tax relief by area and house price decile (1988 £)

House price decile	Total	Birmingham	Bristol	Glasgow	London	Newcastle	Sheffield
0-14,273	340	442	900			260	393
14,273-21,098	364	380	587	485		363	234
21,098-26,630	409	418	540	507		415	279
26,630-32,040	360	318	525	453		309	356
32,040-38,293	418	373	427	309		514	418
38,293-45,497	431	455	465	392	501	417	369
45,497-55,220	511	457	491	699	598	515	432
55,220-67,458	535	403	562	732	579	545	403
67,458-81,951	644	710	631	706	623	753	576
81,951 or higher	678	830	740	598	647	759	545

Note: house price deciles divide at the third decimal place

Table 28

Average mortgage tax relief by age of head of household

Banded age	Average MITR (£)
16-24	575.63
25-44	606.66
45-59	479.61
60 and higher	83.08
Number of cases	**980**

Table 29

Mortgage interest tax relief by distance from city centre (kms)

Distance	Average MITR (£)
0-5 km	524.67
5.01-10 km	559.11
10.01-15 km	635.59
15.01-20 km	657.90
20.01 km or more	623.88
Number of cases	**981**

relief jumps to more than £500 and nearly £700 for houses worth more than £81,950.

Average MITR is shown to vary with age, rising in peak earnings age bands and falling at either end of the age distribution (see **Table 28**). **Table 29** indicates that tax relief rises away from city centres, assisting the suburbs more than the inner cities.

Chapter 1 suggested that the abolition of mortgage interest tax relief in its entirety, with the extra tax rate reducing the PSBR, would bring general interest rates down by two per cent. If the situation of mortgagors with tax relief and 13.3 per cent mortgage interest is compared with a regime of no tax relief but mortgage rates at 11.3 per cent, an approximate calculation can be made of the effects of abolition.

It will lead to an increase of nearly 6 per cent in housing costs for mortgage payers with the largest increases (10.4 per cent and 16 per cent) in Birmingham and Glasgow respectively. The critical variable is the level of interest in operation when tax relief is abolished: the lower the mortgage rate before abolition, the smaller the increase in net mortgage bills. This is not the end of the story, however, as it is

Table 30

Annual mortgage payments before/after tax relief abolition (£)

	With MITR (13.3% gross)	No MITR (11.3% gross)	% increase
Total	**2462**	**2603**	**(5.7)**
Birmingham	**2,165**	**2,390**	**(10.4)**
Bristol	**2,591**	**2,813**	**(8.6)**
Glasgow	**2,180**	**2,530**	**(16.0)**
London	**3,618**	**3,720**	**(2.8)**
Newcastle	**2,071**	**2,134**	**(3.0)**
Sheffield	**1,884**	**1,954**	**(3.7)**

Note: average mortgage payments calculated as (13.3% x outstanding debt) minus MITR, and (11.3% x outstanding debt)

also estimated that house prices could fall by some 7 per cent on average as a result of the abolition of mortgage interest tax relief **(5)**.

In the 1991 Budget, the Chancellor removed the top rate of tax from mortgage interest tax relief provisions, restricting all mortgagors to the MIRAS system. The effect is to insulate the subsidy from the tax system: all mortgagors receive a 25 per cent reduction in their mortgage interest payments up to £30,000. The reduction in tax relief is equivalent to a cut of a third in mortgage interest tax relief for the (previously) top-rate tax payers.

Imputed rental income tax

Until 1963, owner-occupiers paid rental income tax on the rateable value of their property. The purpose of such a tax was to capture the income in kind that owners gained from their asset. Along with the absence of capital gains taxation, this tax expenditure constitutes a subsidy to owners on the investment in their homes: housing stock yields a flow of income and the net return (income net of capital gains) should yield a return at least as good as that available elsewhere.

A rental income tax was simulated to provide estimates of the value and distribution of the tax revenues foregone. This is estimated in the following way. First, the 1988 capital values for the survey stock were calculated (see Appendix 1). Outstanding mortgage debt was subtracted from the estimated capital value, providing a measure of net equity owned by the home owner (since interest payments on the mortgage attract tax relief). The annual income flow is calculated as the net equity multiplied by a rate of return of 4 per cent (to ensure comparability with the calculations elsewhere in this report) and this was then multiplied by the household's marginal tax rate (t) to estimate the value of the subsidy.

Table 31

Average imputed rental income tax, £ per annum

	Value of subsidy	Number of cases
Total	382	3396
Birmingham	323	585
Bristol	445	733
Glasgow	330	398
London	610	574
Newcastle	262	573
Sheffield	291	544

Table 32

Imputed rental income tax by gross income band, £ per annum

	Value of subsidy	Number of cases
0-2,599	417.32	18
2,600-5,199	291.16	65
5,200-7,799	305.85	104
7,800-10,399	291.41	179
10,400-12,999	290.47	247
13,000-15,599	307.83	296
15,600-20,799	374.76	424
20,800-25,999	605.19	257
26,000-31,999	618.81	141
31,200 or more	607.96	150

Table 33

Imputed rental income tax by income band by area (£)

Income band	Birmingham	Bristol	Glasgow	London	Newcastle	Sheffield
0-2,599	255	531	281	671	304	365
2,600-5,199	282	476	295	768	165	209
5,200-7,799	308	341	348	536	223	198
7,800-10,399	254	368	214	572	194	259
10,400-12,999	275	335	237	492	219	252
13,000-15,599	233	335	267	582	149	225
15,600-20,799	277	382	312	654	236	269
20,800-25,999	445	695	481	766	474	500
26,000-31,199	670	589	633	741	485	460
31,200 or more	564	883	513	592	407	547

Tables 5.8 and 5.9 illustrate the patterns of subsidy implied by the absence of an imputed rental income tax. It is evident that the value of the subsidy would not wholly offset mortgage interest tax relief if it was to be added to the present fiscal system. However, it is clear that the higher house-price areas, Bristol and London, enjoy higher levels of the subsidy. Table 32 indicates that, apart from the lowest decile of income (which may contain many elderly outright owners), the profile of the subsidy is flat until the top four deciles where the subsidy increases to a higher level of approximately twice the level of assistance of the other deciles of income. The introduction of such a tax could make the whole system more progressive.

However, when the results are disaggregated by case study area, a very different picture is formed (Table 33). It is much more difficult to identify a pattern, such is the influence of multiple factors pulling the value of the tax expenditure in different directions. For instance, low-income elderly households are likely to receive a significant flow of income from their equity and, at the other end of the scale, younger owners in Bristol and London, despite larger mortgages on their property, enjoy a large income because of the local level of house-price appreciation. In general, regional, demographic and other factors have an important bearing on the value of this particular subsidy.

In Table 34, the imputed subsidy rises with age in the

working years of the household before declining in retirement years. There is a general upward trend, although not uniform, in the extent of the subsidy as location moves outward from the city centre (Table 35).

Table 34

Imputed rental income tax by age of household head

Age of head	Mean subsidy (£)
16-24	**263.34**
25-44	**436.70**
45-59	**484.63**
60 or higher	**340.83**
Number of cases	**1789**

Table 35

Imputed rental income tax by distance from city centre (km)

Distance	Mean subsidy (£)
0-5 km	**393.44**
5.01-10 km	**436.13**
10.01-15 km	**462.60**
15.01-20 km	**517.11**
20 km or more	**468.63**
number of cases	**1792**

Capital gains tax

Since 1982, tax has been levied on the real capital gains made on the sale of assets (but not primary residences). The fact that owner-occupation is not subject to such a tax means that in periods of rapidly fluctuating house prices there is no fiscal restraint on excessive trading in the housing market. The arguments that real gains cannot be made by owner-occupiers does not carry weight in the context of trading-down by more elderly households and also because of equity withdrawal opportunities arising from mortgage deregulation. The American argument that re-cycled capital gains should be tax-exempt whereas only equity withdrawal should be eligible for tax purposes would have been an attractive way forward, if capital gains taxation occurred on an accrual basis; but in Britain capital gains tax only applies when assets are realised. A significant proportion of equity withdrawal occurs not at sale but through re-mortgaging and would therefore be missed by the tax system. British capital gains tax is a light and ineffective tax but it would have a significant impact, nonetheless, if it was applied to primary residences.

The tax is light largely because of the £5,000 annual allowance for each tax unit before any capital gains are taxable but also because of the indexing of purely inflationary capital gains. This is achieved by ignoring any gains made before March 1982 and indexing the intervening period (in the survey's case March 1982 to June 1989): 0 per cent of the nominal gains to March 1982 were taxable rising to 100 per cent of the nominal gains made in the year prior to sale. In effect, the further back towards 1982 the gains were made, the lower the taxable sum from the capital gain. However, this is certainly not equivalent to simply reducing the nominal capital gain by purely inflationary effects;

it in fact yields a greater reduction in taxable capital gains than if the retail price index were applied in the same period. (6)

Table 36 indicates that, even with the restrictions imposed by capital gains tax, households opting to sell in 1988 (who had purchased since 1982) would receive a subsidy of more than £3,400, with Newcastle having the lowest average figure of £2,464 and London, not surprisingly, making the largest of more than £5,000. The distribution indicates a fairly flat distribution of gains between

Table 36

Capital gains subsidy by area, 1988 (£)

	Mean capital gain subsidy assuming sale in 1988	Number of cases
Total	3403	2189
Birmingham	2969	384
Bristol	3677	460
Glasgow	3356	294
London	5034	342
Newcastle	2465	339
Sheffield	2903	370

Table 37

Capital gains tax subsidy by banded income, 1988 (£)

Income (£)	Mean capital gain subsidy assuming 1988 sale	number of cases
0-2,599	3455	28
2,600-5,199	2645	94
5,200-7,799	2937	90
7,800-10,399	2499	115
10,400-12,999	2888	145
13,000-15,599	3078	168
15,600-20,799	3456	243
20,800-25,999	4699	150
26,000-31,199	5545	86
31,200 or more	4330	82

Table 38

Mean capital gains tax subsidy by income band by area, 1988 (£)

Income band	Birmingham	Bristol	Glasgow	London	Newcastle	Sheffield
0-2,599	2125	4582	3431	4986	1734	3158
2,600-5,199	2744	3433	2453	3683	1857	1931
5,200-7,799	2846	2928	3901	3796	2419	1760
7,800-10,399	2129	3062	2003	4379	2166	2139
10,400-12,999	2342	2997	2495	5087	2537	2640
13,000-15,599	2610	3224	3266	4332	2415	2475
15,600-20,799	2929	3877	3126	4461	2531	3257
20,800-25,999	4283	5052	3468	5663	3233	5179
26,000-31,199	5878	3926	6534	7303	3402	4296
31,200 or more	3501	5271	3552	4397	3522	6351

incomes of between £2,600 and £15,599 (**Table 37**), before a rise in the subsidy up to the ninth decile before there is another decline among those with the highest incomes. The higher level of subsidy for households in the lowest income band may reflect the position of elderly owner occupiers, typically outright owners who have substantial real capital gains tied to up in their homes.

The regional profile of the distribution of capital gains subsidies is indicated in **Table 38**. They do not rise evenly with income; their distribution is U-shaped in the same way as the aggregate case. As one might expect, there is a strong association between the level of capital gains tax exemption and property prices. In **Table 39**, the average tax concession shows a strong relationship with house prices; it is nine times larger in the top decile in house prices compared with the bottom.

Capital gains exemption declines by age band (with the exception of those aged between 16 and 24 - **Table 40**). Although the subsidy declines within the first three bands of 5 km from the city centre (**Table 41**), capital gains tax subsidy leaps by a third in the fourth distance band.

Supporting home ownership

Table 39
Capital gains tax subsidy by banded 1988 property values (£)

Price range	Mean subsidy
0 - 14273	577
1,4273 - 2,1098	875
2,1098 - 2,6630	1064
2,6630 - 3,2040	1593
3,2040 - 3,8293	1892
3,8293 - 4,5497	2245
4,5497 - 5,5220	2974
5,5220 - 6,7458	3781
6,7458 - 8,1951	4194
8,1951 or higher	5201
Total	**3404**
Number of cases	**2189**

Table 40
Capital gains tax exemption by age of household head, 1988 (£)

Age band	Mean subsidy (£)
16-24	3305.83
25-44	3562.06
45-59	3189.78
60 and higher	2881.74
number of cases	**2183**

Table 41
Capital gains tax by distance from city centre (km), 1988 (£)

Distance	Mean subsidy (£)
0-5 km	3425.77
5.01-10 km	3396.90
10.01-15 km	2993.56
15.01-20 km	4049.07
20.01 km or more	3544.00
Number of cases	**2189**

Council house sales

The single largest subsidy per household is for council house tenants who exercise the Right to Buy. The purchase price is discounted from an assessor's valuation on the basis of a formula that increases the discount in proportion to the length of the household's tenancy and is more favourable for flats than for houses. Since 1980, over 1.3 million council houses have been sold into owner-occupation (7). In the household survey, there were more than 400 Right-to-Buy cases.

Table 42

Level of Right-to-Buy discount by case-study area (1988 prices) (£)

	Average	Discount cases
Total	**12094**	**420**
Birmingham	**9211**	**62**
Bristol	**12816**	**54**
Glasgow	**12639**	**85**
London	**21675**	**59**
Newcastle	**8650**	**78**
Sheffield	**9618**	**82**

Note: these figures are based on 1988 prices for all valid survey cases from 1980 to 1988.

Table 42 indicates the average discount (in 1988 prices) for ex-tenants who bought between 1980 and 1988 (inclusive). The regional differentials are large, ranging from £8,650 in Newcastle to £21,675 in London, but the average subsidy in the form of the tenancy-related discount for all cases is in excess of £12,000. This is a remarkable level of subsidy, unparalleled in the UK housing finance system. The extent of these subsidies are further illustrated in **Table 43** at a disaggregated level, indicating the regional disparity with large levels of subsidy in low house-price regions as well as London and Bristol.

Table 43

Value of Right-to-Buy discount by area, 1980-88, (1988 prices) (£)

Year	Birmingham	Bristol	Glasgow	London	Newcastle	Sheffield
1980	**10,870**	**14,770**	**14,219**	**18,038**	**13,733**	
1981	**11,619**	**11,799**	**10,135**	**16,672**	**9,699**	**9,618**
1982	**9,625**	**10,862**	**12,189**	**16,099**	**8,244**	**9,762**
1983	**9,304**	**10,754**	**10,764**	**19,656**	**7,534**	**9,849**
1984	**7,443**	**16,755**	**13,909**	**15,271**	**7,832**	**9,299**
1985	**9,283**	**10,294**	**12,185**	**22,534**	**8,931**	**7,888**
1986	**7,746**	**10,884**	**12,459**	**23,022**	**7,330**	**8,210**
1987	**9,817**	**15,753**	**13,701**	**28,965**	**8,978**	**7,903**
1988	**9,395**	**17,215**	**13,130**	**28,259**	**8,989**	**10,984**

Supporting home ownership

Table 44

Average percentage Right-to-Buy discount 1980-88

	Average discount %	Cases
Total	**46.6**	**420**
Birmingham	**41.5**	**62**
Bristol	**47.2**	**54**
Glasgow	**50.7**	**85**
London	**47.4**	**59**
Newcastle	**44.4**	**78**
Sheffield	**47.4**	**82**

Note: these figures give the average percentage discount for all valid survey cases from 1980 to 1988.

Table 45

Average capital gain by Right-to-Buy purchasers 1980-1988, (1988 prices) (£)

	Average capital gain	Cases
Total	**16,764.76**	**458**
Birmingham	**15,601.15**	**68**
Bristol	**19,872.86**	**66**
Glasgow	**19,301.82**	**89**
London	**14,275.17**	**61**
Newcastle	**15,921.17**	**84**
Sheffield	**15,330.54**	**90**

Note: these average values were calculated by subtracting the discounted purchase price (in 1988 prices) from the estimated 1988 lower market values.

In **Table 44** the percentage discount received by ex-tenant purchasers was averaged over the period 1980-88. This indicates that average discounts were 46.4 per cent of the undiscounted price, higher in Glasgow, primarily due to the large number of flats which receive a higher percentage discount.

Table 45 calculates the capital appreciation of Right-to-Buy properties bought between 1980-1988 on the basis of their estimated 1988 value (using the lower-

Table 46

Right-to-Buy discount (£) by gross banded income (1988 Prices)

	Mean discount	Number of cases
0-2599	**14,864**	**8**
2,600-5199	**11,809**	**31**
5,200-7799	**13`,183**	**35**
7,800-10399	**12,056**	**34**
10,400-12999	**9,760**	**38**
13,000-15599	**10,273**	**27**
15,600-20799	**12,475**	**44**
20,800-25999	**13,916**	**12**
26,000-31199	**16,785**	**6**
31,200 or more	**19,018**	**4**
Average	**12,123**	**239**

value estimates, see chapter 3) minus the discounted purchase price (in 1988 prices). The average capital gain for the study as a whole was almost £17,000, falling to less than £14,500 in London but as large as £19,872 in Bristol. London values can be reconciled as lower than Glasgow, for example, because the discount factor for flats, so prevalent in Glasgow, must have offset the capital gains made in the last decade by Londoners. By any measure these are remarkable levels of gain for the ex-tenants of the survey.

Table 47

Right-to-Buy capital gain (£) by house price deciles (1988 Values)

House price decile	Discount	Number of cases
0-23,572	12,951.74	19
23,572-25481	14,085.48	48
25,481-27199	15,741.11	101
27,199-29083	17,011.32	51
29,083-31000	18,080.87	54
31,000-32998	18,315.86	61
32,998-35368	18,311.30	52
35,368-37797	18,602.53	44
37,797-41699	14,868.99	24
41,699 or higher	19,364.12	4

Note: house price deciles are split on the third decimal point.

Table 46 examines the actual value of the Right-to-Buy discount by gross banded income (remembering that subsidy here depends on length of tenancy and whether the property is a flat or a house). The table indicates that the discount takes on a distinctive U-shaped pattern with respect to income. Finally, **Table 47** sets the capital gain made against the estimated current (1988) value of the property. Again, as one would expect, the subsidy rises in proportion with higher house prices, although not smoothly. The first five deciles climb steadily from around £13,000, rising to more than £18,000. After the fifth decile, with one exception, capital gain remains fairly constant.

Property taxes

Until recent years, the use of a property tax to fund local government finance acted to correct some of the tax concessions enjoyed by homeowners. As a tax on the consumption of housing, domestic rates substituted for Value Added Tax. Alternatively, as a tax on capital, the property tax acted as a crude wealth tax. However, the rateable value-based tax was poorly related to income and problems with revaluation and local government spending conspired to put the abolition of rates on the agenda.

In 1991, just one year after its introduction in England and Wales (after two years in Scotland), the community charge is to be abolished and replaced by a new 'council tax' which will combine elements of a property tax with a personal tax. The choice of a new tax is formidably complex, raising questions about structure, the constitution and public expenditure, as well as the impact of any new taxes on householders (8).

In this section, a very crude simulation of a new capital value tax is attempted, which uses 1988-89 average gross rates bills as a benchmark along with estimates of market value. Such a tax would have no poll tax element. These figures provide an estimate of the burdens implied by such a tax, were it to be introduced.

This simulation adopts some strong assumptions: it is revenue-neutral (that is, a tax that raises the same revenue as the previous tax) and, therefore, there are no specific grants to assist regions with excessive household tax bills because of the level of house prices in their area. It is also assumed that there is 100 per cent take-up of housing benefit. These figures should, as a result, carry a strong statistical 'health warning'.

Table 48 summarises the calculations made to generate property tax rates for the five major city councils in the study. On the assumption that the number of cases accurately represent the distribution of property values in each city authority, the technique adopted used Sheffield as an example. Average rates for 1988-89 (£452.39) multiplied by the number of cases (1,456) provides an estimate of the sample revenue required for any revenue-neutral form of local taxation (£658,679). At the same time, the number of adults in these sample housing groups totals 2,499 and the total sample market value is in the region of £30,966. On such a revenue-neutral basis, a poll tax for Sheffield in 1988-89, from this sample technique, can be estimated as equal to the revenue divided by the number of adults, or £264. The property tax rate is simply the revenue divided by total market value (1.463%).

Table 49 indicates the distribution of the burden of the capital value tax for the five cities according to average gross tax payments by tenure. Tables 50 and 51 conflate the results to indicate the distributional and tenure-specific implications of net and gross tax bills under such a new tax. With five cities, there is a disproportionate number of council tenants and, accordingly, of households with low income. This

Table 48

Calculating a revenue-neutral local tax (£), 1988-9

	Sheffield	Newcastle	Birmingham	Bristol	Glasgow
Average rates	452.39	444.76	480.96	473.32	506
No. of cases	1456	592	1070	982	907
No. of adults	2499	993	1815	1730	1142
Mean market value	30906	31558	40866	51596	36353
Revenue	658679	263298	514627	464800	458942
Poll tax	264	265	284	269	402
(%) Tax rate	1.463	1.412	1.176	0.917	1.392

Table 49

Distribution of new property tax by tenure, 1988-9 prices (£), five cities (gross payments)

	Sheffield	Newcastle	Birmingham	Bristol	Glasgow
Owner occupier	588.31	609.82	571.94	542.69	645.78
Local authority	274.18	304.73	313.91	345.59	440.40
Housing assn	297.80	283.03	368.08	293.84	466.83
Private renting	397.68	378.99	417.99	396.84	506.18

means that in net terms, tax payments would tend to the maximum 80 per cent rebate for those households with incomes below £5,200. Net local taxes are premised on a housing benefit system that gives up to 80 per cent rebates with a taper of benefit withdrawal set at 15 per cent. The property tax would have a striking

positive relationship with income both in terms of gross and net payments. Average local authority taxes are about 60 per cent of gross payments by owners. If such a tax is placed alongside the subsidies received by home-owners, it would make a major contribution to reducing tenure bias in terms of subsidy assistance.

Table 50
Distribution of new property tax by tenure and gross income

Tenure	(£ mean)	(cases)
Owner-occupier	581.63	2576
Local authority	341.78	1880
Housing association	365.25	161
Private rented	411.14	390
Total	471.33	5007

Income band		
0-2,599	329.91	640
2,600-5,199	377.17	936
5,200-7,799	430.41	338
7,800-10,399	461.49	258
10,400-12,999	500.48	241
13,000-15,599	500.43	196
15,600-20,799	561.32	246
20,800-25,999	685.82	121
26,000-31,199	748.59	44
31,200 or more	869.05	57

Table 51
Distribution of new property tax by net payments

Tenure	(£ mean)	(cases)
Owner-occupier	536.25	2576
Local authority	183.18	1880
Housing association	225.29	161
Private renting	262.44	390
Total	372.35	5007

Income band		
0-2599	10.58	640
2600-5199	106.88	936
5,200-7,799	348.76	338
7,800-10,399	441.14	258
10,400-12,999	487.72	241
13,000-15,599	500.07	196
15,600-20,799	561.32	246
20,800-25,999	685.82	121
26,000-31,199	748.59	44
31,200 or more	869.05	57

Conclusions

The results of the survey aptly demonstrate the extent and variation of the support home-owners receive from the the tax system. Particularly in terms of capital gains (although very volatile) and the discount afforded to council house sales, there is no parallel in terms of generosity. But the generosity extends further: nowhere else is such a level of subsidy meted out with so little thought for its distribution, its cost and its consequences. Whether mortgage interest tax relief or the investment aspects of income and capital gain are considered, the subsidy received is extraordinarily badly targeted; it sits uncomfortably beside the narrow comfort of housing benefit received by public and private tenants.

Most taxation experts agree that capital gains taxation is not an effective tax but the housing policy arguments against levying such a tax are unconvincing at a time of considerable housing market instability and in the light of the macro-economic consequences of mortgage deregulation. A tax on housing, be it locally or nationally based, is a fundamental first corrective to the privileged position of the home-owner. The abolition of top-rate tax relief on mortgage interest payments and the return of some form of local property tax are the beginning of such a movement.

6 Conclusions

Changes in housing taxation and subsidy arrangements could enhance economic growth, distribute assistance more fairly and encourage greater efficiency in the provision of housing.

A radical, phased reduction in the overall value of tax subsidies to housing would do much to ensure real stability in house prices well into the 1990s. The introduction of taxation on imputed rental income and housing capital gains are unlikely political possibilities. As a substitute, the re-introduction of a property tax, if it is closely related to capital values of dwellings, and the phased abolition of mortgage interest tax relief, would be suitable alternatives. Such changes will also require supplementation by measures to reduce lags in the supply of housing as a result of price rises. Government must regard rising real house prices across the nation as a problem requiring political action, with credit controls a last resort.

Reductions in tax assistance to home-owners, especially those on above-average incomes, could also enhance the fairness of subsidy arrangements. **Table 52** indicates that, at incomes above £5,200 per annum, the subsidies received by owners, whether this is measured by mortgage interest tax relief alone or the sum of capital gains and exemptions from imputed rental income tax, exceed those received by tenants in all of the rental sectors.

The phasing out of mortgage interest tax relief will still leave owners favoured as long as house-price gains remain untaxed. Rents in the social sector, raised on an appropriate valuation basis, need to be 'historically weighted' if owners and renters are to be fairly treated. Such weightings yield rents in the social sector which would imply only modest increases in housing benefit; and they would produce rent-to-income ratios in the range of 20-25 per cent of average earnings. If inflation is reduced to low levels and remains low the 'historic weighting factor' would become negligible in the long run.

An all-embracing pricing policy for the rental sector is impossible to devise with the likely future tax arrangements for owner-occupation. Private rental tenants are relatively unsubsidised by government and overall subsidies to private tenants are low. If the government wishes to expand this sector further, there should be a tax concession, preferably in the form of a depreciation allowance, for landlords letting in a mobility-oriented sector; this would be a substitute for owner-occupation rather than social housing. Private landlords wishing to invest in housing for low-income

Table 52

Subsidy by tenure and gross income

| Income | Home owners | | | Local authority | | Housing Associations | |
	MITR	CGT *	IR	Rent distortion	HB	Rent distortion	HB
2600	191	494	417	356	726	192	649
2600-5199	126	378	291	321	612	289	486
5200-7799	284	420	306	291	323	406	180
7800-10399	300	357	291	247	64	261	109
10400-12999	405	413	290	358	23		
13000-15599	440	440	308	281	20		
15600-20799	488	494	375				
20800-25999	748	671	605				
26000-31199	888	792	619				
31200	1002	619	608				

| Income | Private rented housing | | | |
| | Registered rental | | Unregistered rental | |
	Rent distortion	HB	Rent distortion	HB
2600	197	472	350	222
2600-5199	321	346	189	344
5200-7799	18	198	-73	231
7800-10399	245	51	-134	256
10400-12999	156	10	-639	160

* Capital gains tax exemption annualised over the seven year period of 1982-88.

Conclusions

groups, and competing with the social sector, should have access to tenure-neutral capital grants but in return be licensed and have approved tenancy arrangements. Tenure-neutrality in awarding capital grants would have to consider the difficulties in recouping windfall surpluses from private landlords and the unlikelihood that historic weightings could be applied in the private sector.

Consistent, two-part and capital-value-based rents in the social sector would facilitate a fairer distribution of housing benefit. It is unlikely that the government will reform radically the scale and structure of the present scheme, although the dual-taper scheme proposed by Hills (1) has our full support. In the longer term, it is hoped that the advocates of a higher 'basic income' will be listened to by government and this would reduce the traps and gaps between the tax and benefit systems.

The broad framework of legislation for the rental sector in Britain offers opportunities to create an expanded, diversified sector. Nobody wants to return to a monopoly of municipal landlordism nor to Rachmanism. But the 1988 Housing Acts do require a supportive, efficient framework of finance and subsidies. Until now there has been a belief, often implicit,

that rents which were more closely aligned to those of the market-place, together with a reduction in subsidies to housing producers, could achieve the objectives of housing policy by letting the housing benefit system take the strain. Even with reduced tax subsidies to owners and reduced house-price inflation, such a framework is unlikely to produce the housing output required at rents which can be sustained by those in employment.

A realistic and economic approach to providing a supportive financial framework could emerge with consistent rent-setting, adequate and competitively available capital grants, and an efficient channel for private finance to flow into social housing.

There is a case for public housing investment in Britain if its citizens are to be well-housed, neighbourhoods upgraded and the quality of cities and villages enhanced. The required investment, however, must trigger rational rather than unfair patterns of subsidy; neither private nor public spending should damage the trade-off between growth and inflation which will be vital to securing a prosperous Britain in the 21st century.

Appendices

Appendix 1
Estimating market values:
hedonic estimation and results

We found it necessary to estimate market values where no direct valuations exist. To do so, we made full use of the Joseph Rowntree Foundation data-set.

A great deal of the housing stock is not traded (social housing) or traded infrequently (private housing). The technique chosen to derive market values is the hedonic approach, a technique familiar to housing and urban economists (1). Before describing the method and the results of the present estimation from the JRF data, this note summarises the general principles, strengths and weaknesses of the technique.

The basic idea behind the use of the hedonic approach is that housing consists of attributes which are the fundamental source of housing demand. The algebraic sum of these attributes - normally consisting of structural, neighbourhood and locational variables: the number of rooms, floorspace, garage etc, weighted by their implicit price, generates the market value of the property. Thus the underlying demand and supply for these attributes determines the traded price.

There are a number of key assumptions required for the hedonic technique:

- The market for each of these attributes is in 'unitary equilibrium', i.e there are no sub-markets among the data.
- The list of hedonic variables used is comprehensive.
- The functional form of the equation is correctly specified; for example, a linear relationship maybe assumed in the model but may not be the true relationship between the housing attributes.

These are strong assumptions, notably the last one. It is because the attributes have their price determined by their own supply and demand functions that we cannot *a priori* determine the functional form to take. This is an empirical question with an undoubted degree of arbitrariness involved. There are functional form estimators (the 'Box-and-Cox' technique) which can shed some light. Numerically, most equations take a log-log or semi-log functional form, although Hancock found a linear model performed best on the Glasgow 'travel-to-work-area' data (see Appendix 3 of the Glasgow Case Study).

These models are not without justifiable weakness; they offer one specific way to measure property values

Appendices

Table 53
Hedonic regression results on JRF survey data 1983-88, all regions (£)

Variables	Description	Entire market	Bottom half	Top half
1987		-11967	-4823	-19686
1986		-15901	-6774	-24574
1985		-25067	-8499	-39931
1984		-25344	-9722	-40668
1983		-29854	-11116	-45866
Birmingham		10742	2483	17977
Bristol		15209	6744	15101
Glasgow		15116	5799	11244*
London		59564	11474	65633
Newcastle		-	-	-
Hage1	pre1919	-	-1970	-
Hage2	1919-44	-2959*	-1057	-
Largekit	large kitchen	3435*	1007**	8441*
Garden		-7045	-1179*	-11514**
Garage		5556	3175	7289**
Htype1	detached	18051	7492	15813
Htype2	semi-terrace	-	3177	-
Commerce	commercial area	-	3244**	-
Graffiti	serious problem	-3672*	-2581	-
Goodbldg	equal/better > area	-	-	-
Logapts	habitable room	83493	5993	124632
Centheat	central heating	2454	800	5127**
Logbath	per bathroom	17047	1196**	31367
Logdble	per room	-	-	-
Logcbd	km from city centre	-15193	-	-33131
Logimmig	proportion of immigrants	-	-	-
Constant		189+	17955	-6096+

Continued over ...

Table 53 *continued*

Hedonic regression results on JRF survey data 1983-88, all regions (£)

Variables	Description	Entire market	Bottom half	Top half
R2		0.42	0.51	0.37
F		71.3	48.1	33.4
Cases		1929	971	958
DW		1.91	1.65	1.93

- = eliminated

+ = insig. on constant term

* = sig. to 0.1

** = sig. to 0.05

otherwise significant to 0.001

Note: years represent time dummies with default set at 1988.

***Hage** refers to period of construction.*

***Largekit** refers to presence of a large kitchen*

***Garden/garage** - refers to their presence*

***Htype** refers to property type*

***Commerce** refers to location in commercial area*

***Grafitti** refers to problem of graffiti in the area*

***Goodbldg** refers to property being better or as good as area*

***Logimmig** refers to the percentage of immigrants in the area*

*The prefix "**log**" indicates that the variable was entered in log form*

but they are questionable. This will become more apparent as we discuss the techniques used by the central team to estimate market values on all properties. We took all purchases of property recorded in the survey from 1983 to 1988 (excluding Right to Buy and other non-traded acquisitions) which amounted to 1,929 valid cases. We then constructed a log-linear regression on price for these cases with a set of independent variables which can be divided between dummy or dichotomous variables and logged continuous variables. The parameter values of the dummies and the anti-log values of the other variables are then treated as the marginal price of the attributes in question.

Thus in **Table 53**, for the market as a whole, the regional premium for living in London (as opposed to the default case of Sheffield) is nearly £60,000. The price of an additional habitable room is £8,349. These implicit prices then become weights which can be applied to form market values on the rest of the stock. Using the backward elimination regression technique, all variables that failed to reach 0.10 significance were excluded, in practice for the market as a whole, this meant dropping six out of more than 25 variables. There was some colinearity between HTYPE1 and HTYPE2 but elsewhere it was virtually absent.

We chose to repeat the regression on the bottom half and the top half of the traded stock because we felt that the quality and value of social housing stock may well be more accurately reflected by the lower half of the housing market than by the market as a whole. This is very rough and ready, but the results show striking differences with equally important implications for policy, eg market rents. The market value suggested by the weights drawn from the entire market sample is called MARVAL. For the lower half only, the result is called LOWVAL and for the upper half, UPPERVAL. **Table 54** reproduces the mean MARVAL results for each tenure and region.

Table 54
Estimated mean capital values (MARVAL)

Region	All	OO	LA	HA	PR
Birmingham	39566	47917	22555	30933	34910
Bristol	53160	59405	35653	31598	42304
Glasgow	36994	49638	28372	33373	34556
London	78869	83947	70321	71883	73113
Newcastle	28902	38215	18039	17164	20733
Sheffield	31306	40178	18432	21586	27834
ALL	44263				

Appendix 2:

Consequences for housing benefit
of proposed reforms

Much of the analysis in this report has been concerned with the subsidy implicit in, for instance, local authority rents compared with some measure of market rents. While it is relatively straightforward to calculate gross market rents from estimated capital values (given assumptions about rates of return, depreciation, and management and maintenance allowances) this tells us nothing about the net impact on households of market rents or of the level of subsidy. The housing benefit system modifies housing cost and local tax burdens by 100 per cent on the margin, operating with reference to the income support system under the basic formulae:

$$\text{HB (rents)} = R - 0.65 \, (Y\text{-}A)$$

and

$$\text{HB (rates)} = 0.8T - 0.20 \, (Y\text{-}A)$$
$$\text{HB (poll tax)} = 0.8T - 0.15 \, (Y\text{-}A)$$

where R equals gross rents, T is local tax, 0.65 (and 0.2 and 0.15 for local taxes) is the taper of benefit reduction, Y is net income and A is the household's applicable amount calculated with reference to the Income Support system; that is, the allowances calculated by the State to determine Income Support requirements which depend on household size, age and special needs. (Note that, as of 1988-89, maximum rebates for local taxes were 80 per cent and not 100 per cent, as with rent rebates.) If net income is less than or equal to the relevant applicable amount, benefit is either 100 per cent of rents or 80 per cent of local taxes. Thereafter, as income rises, benefit is withdrawn at a constant fraction (0.65 for rents) for every pound of additional income.

For the purposes of investigating the net effects of market rents and of re-introducing a property tax, a basic simulation of the housing benefit system was developed. The key variables required were an estimate of the household's applicable amount and the calculated variable, net income. These restrictions allowed 5,500 usable cases or 58 per cent of all cases in the survey. Applicable amounts were calculated by assigning all housing groups to a household type and then using the housing benefit applicable amounts for 1988-89, scaled up to annual levels, to provide an estimate of annual net income proposed by the State to be the allowance level for each household type.

For the 80 per cent of cases that fit into 'simple' household types, it was straightforward to provide a

Appendices

Table 55

Household types for housing benefit model

	% of total	(N)
Single elderly	**14.7**	**1405**
Couple elderly	**13.0**	**1241**
Single adult	**10.5**	**1006**
Couple adult	**15.8**	**1507**
Lone parent	**4.4**	**420**
Couple with children	**21.2**	**2031**
Other	**20.4**	**1951**

weight based on the annual value of their applicable amount. For the remaining 20 per cent, the position was radically simplified by assuming there are two adult households in these remaining cases. Other assumptions employed were that net income calculated from the survey was equivalent to net income for housing benefit purposes; that households were the same as housing groups; and that children were aged below 11 for benefit purposes. The effect of capital and other disregards in the calculation of benefit entitlement were ignored and it was assumed that take-up of benefit is 100 per cent.

Benefit entitlement

The first exercise conducted was to ascertain the proportion of households in each tenure and region who were entitled to 100 per cent housing benefit on rents or housing costs or 80 per cent of local taxes.

The most striking figures contrast the proportions eligible for full benefit between tenure, not between regions. For the regions as a whole, Bristol has only 16 per cent of cases but Glasgow has nearly 27 per cent, relative to the aggregate average of 22 per cent of cases eligible for full support. These variations are small compared with the 7 per cent of owners who fit the eligibility criteria as against 38 per cent of local authority tenants. Figures for associations and private tenants are less robust, but the high level of cases among private and association tenants in Birmingham is striking.

Housing benefit consequences of pricing reforms
The remaining tables, **57** to **59**, illustrate the consequences for housing benefit, in terms of expenditure increases and additional recipients, of moving from current rent-setting mechanisms (1988-89) to the proposed version of historically-weighted market rents. **Table 57** indicates the average housing benefit costs of the present system of rents in the rented sectors in the survey.

Table 56

Entitlement to maximum housing benefit, percentage, by tenure and area

	Total	Birmingham	Bristol	Glasgow	London	Newcastle	Sheffield	Cases
Total	22.6	25.7	16.1	26.7	19.2	21.8	25.4	5504
Owner	6.8	7.4	5.7	5.8	7.7	6.5	7.9	2662
LA	38.0	45.2	37.0	35.6	36.1	34.6	42.2	2315
HA	30.8	41.2	25.0	18.2	28.6	33.3	35.3	159
PRS	33.8	51.5	36.2	29.2	27.3	31.4	26.6	408

Table 57

Average housing benefit using current rents
by tenure and area

	(£)	Number of cases
Local authority	827.80	1142
Housing association	874.56	72
Private renting	921.37	174
Birmingham	817.51	197
Bristol	844.37	159
Glasgow	649.61	265
London	1038.89	162
Newcastle	870.80	337
Sheffield	893.35	268
Total	841.95	1388

It is clear that there is more variation in housing benefit expenditure by region than there is by tenure. In particular, it is interesting to note that housing benefit expenditure is highest among private tenants and lowest among local authority tenants. London has by far the highest level of spending, Glasgow much the lowest.

In **Table 58**, it is assumed that rents are introduced in the social sector using the bottom half of market values, weighted by the the 'historic factor' prevailing in each of the six areas. Housing benefit expenditure will rise by an average of 6.1 per cent for the survey as a whole. However, housing association benefit expenditure will

Appendices

Table 58

Average housing benefit (low-weighted market rent, 4% return)

	(£)	(N)	£ mean % increase	number
Local authority	891.85	1654	7.7	44.8
Housing association	822.59	108	-6.0	50.0
Private renting	934.27	232	1.4	33.3
Birmingham	914.89	283	11.9	43.6
Bristol	987.61	222	17.0	39.6
Glasgow	903.19	470	39.0	77.4
London	950.56	225	-8.5	38.9
Newcastle	827.56	435	-5.0	29.1
Sheffield	852.22	378	-5.6	41.0
Total	893.61	2013	6.1	45.0

Note: figures for total cases and each region (but not tenure) include 19 lodgers/boarders

actually fall relative to the present situation. London and Newcastle also face lower bills but Glasgow faces a rise in benefit expenditure of 39 per cent. In relation to number of recipients, the figures are very different, with 45 per cent more households becoming eligible as a whole, with as many as 77 per cent more cases becoming eligible in Glasgow to 29 per cent in Newcastle.

In **Table 59** the situation is replicated using low market values (ie with higher rents based on 5.5 per cent returns instead of 4 per cent used in the previous case). This implies a 29.1 per cent increase in housing benefit expenditure compared with the present system. Under this regime, all housing organisations and all regions face higher housing benefit bills, notably so for Glasgow at 71 per cent more than under

Table 59

Average housing benefit (low-weighted market rent, 5.5% return)

	(£)	N	£	N
	Mean		% increase	
Local authority	1,088.83	1726	31.5	51.1
Housing association	114.62	113	16.0	56.9
Private renting	1,102.68	249	19.7	43.1
Birmingham	1,102.79	296	34.9	50.2
Bristol	1,219.35	231	44.4	45.3
Glasgow	1,110.07	492	70.9	85.7
London	1,140.83	239	9.8	47.5
Newcastle	998.64	459	14.7	36.2
Sheffield	1,037.87	91	16.2	45.9
Total	1086.86	2108	29.1	51.9

Note: total and regions include 20 lodgers/boarders cases.

the current regime and 10 per cent for London. Local authorities as a whole face the largest expenditure increase at 31.5 per cent. All organisations and all regions face disproportionately larger increases in the number of recipients, averaging 52 per cent for all areas, rising from 36 per cent in Newcastle to 85 per cent in Glasgow. Housing associations face the largest eligibility increase of housing landlords.

References

Preface

Hills J, *Thirty-nine steps to housing finance reform*, Joseph Rowntree Foundation, 1991.

Chapter 1

1   Fleming M C and Nellis J G, 'The Rise and Fall of House Prices: Causes, Consequences and Prospects', *National Westminster Bank Quarterly Review*, November 1990.

2   Coombes M and Raybould S, *Housing Research Findings No 30*, Joseph Rowntree Foundation, March 1991.

3   Muellbauer J and Murphy A, *House prices and migration*, Shearson Lehman and Hutton Securities Research Report, December 1988.

4   Pannell R, 'Trends in the Personal Sector Balance Sheet', *Housing Finance*, No.8, Council of Mortgage Lenders, November 1990.

5   Lomax J, 'Housing finance - an international perspective', *Bank of England Quarterly Bulletin*, February 1991.

6   Maclennan D and Munro M, 'The growth of owner-occupation in Britain : emerging context and research issues' in Booth, P and Crook, A (eds.) *Low Cost Home Ownership: an Evaluation of Housing Policy Under the Conservatives*, Gower, 1986.

7   Muellbauer J, *The Great British Housing Disaster and Economic Policy*, Institute for Public Policy Research, Economic Study Number 5, 1990.

8   Ball M, *Filling the void: a research agenda on housing construction*, mimeo, Joseph Rowntree Foundation, 1991.

9   Lowe S and Watson S, *From First-Time Buyers to Last-Time Sellers: an Appraisal of the Social and Economic Consequences of Equity Withdrawal from the Housing Market*, University of York, 1990.

10 Costello J and Coles A, 'The Housing Market and the Wider Economy', *Housing Finance*, No. 9, Council for Mortgage Lenders, February 1991.

11 Ermisch J, *Fewer Babies, Longer Lives*, Joseph Rowntree Foundation, 1990.

12 Wilcox S, *Macro-economic implications of removing mortgage interest tax relief*, mimeo, Joseph Rowntree Foundation, 1991.

13 Hutton W, 'Ending the Big Lend', *Roof*, March/April, 1991.

Chapter 2

1 Department of the Environment, *Annual Report, The Government's Expenditure Plans 1991-92 to 1993-94*, cm 1508, 1991.

2 Kleinman M, *A Decade of Change: Providing Social Housing, 1980-1990*, mimeo, Joseph Rowntree Foundation, 1991.

3 Hills J, *Unravelling Housing Finance*, Oxford University Press, 1991.

4 Maclennan D, Gibb K and More, A, *Paying for Britain's Housing*, Joseph Rowntree Foundation, 1990.

5 Maclennan D and Kearns A, *Public Finance for Housing in Britain*, Centre for Housing Research Discussion Paper 22, University of Glasgow, 1989.

6 Maclennan et al, *op.cit.*, 1990.

7 Maclennan D, Clapham D, Goodlad R, Kemp, P, Malcolm J, Satsangi M and Whitefield L, *The Nature and Effectiveness of Housing Management in England: A Report to the Department of the Environment*, HMSO, 1989.

8 Kleinman M, *op. cit.*, 1991.

Chapter 3

1 Hills J, *Unravelling Housing Finance*, Oxford University Press, 1991.

2 Bramley G, Bartlett W, Franklin A and Lambert C, *Housing Finance and the Housing Market in Bristol*, Joseph Rowntree Foundation, 1990.

3 See Hills J, *op. cit.* (1991) for a justification of this approach.

Chapter 4

1 Kleinman M , *op. cit*, 1991.

2 House of Commons, Session, Committee of Public Accounts, *27th Report, Housing Association Grant and Housing Needs and Allocations*, HMSO, 1989-90.

3 Kearns A, 'Housing Policy, Deprivation and Space : the case of stress areas', *Policy and Politics*, Vol 18, no.2, 1990.

References

4 Bramley G, *Meeting Housing Needs*, Association of District Councils, 1989.

5 See National and Welsh Federations of Housing Associations' *'CORE' Bulletins*; Scottish Federation of Housing Associations/Scottish Homes, *The SCORE system: the early start scheme in the Tayside, Grampian and Fife Regions*, Scottish Homes Research Report Number 14, 1990; Department of the Environment, *New Lettings by Housing Associations*, HMSO, 1990.

6 The JRF household survey generated small samples of association tenants and the results in this section should be used with caution, even though the socio-economic profile is similar to national studies. As the JRF survey in 1988/89 pre-dated changes to the association funding systems an attempt has been made to update estimates of subsidy levels using other data sources.

7 Maclennan D, 'Resident Benefits, Spillover and Expectations in a Housing Revitalisation Programme' in Satsangi, M (ed) *Changing Housing Finance Systems: Studies in Housing 4*, Centre for Housing Research, University of Glasgow, 1990.

8 More A, *The New Financial Regime for Housing Associations: An initial assessment of the impact of the new funding system on housing association and housing co-operative activity in Scotland*, A Report to Scottish Homes, January 1991.

9 Duckworth S, 'How Housing Associations look to Private Lenders', *Voluntary Housing*, September 1990.

10 More A, *op.cit.*, 1991.

11 Couttie D, *Increasing institutional investment for rented housing*, Joseph Rowntree Foundation, 1991.

12 Whitehead C, and Pryke M, 'Private finance for social housing: enabling or transforming?', *Housing Research Findings No 24*, Joseph Rowntree Foundation, January 1991.

13 Kemp P and Crook A, 'The impact of the Business Expansion Scheme on the provision of rented housing', *Housing Research Findings No. 29*, Joseph Rowntree Foundation, 1991.

14 Sharp C, 'Homelessness, housing benefit and the private rented sector', *Housing Research Findings No. 28*, Joseph Rowntree Foundation, March 1991.

15 'Gro-Grants' are capital grants for rent and ownership.

Chapter 5

1 Muellbauer J, *op. cit.*, 1990.

2 Atkinson A and King M, 'Housing Policy, Taxation and Reform', *Midland Bank Review*, Spring, pp. 7-15, 1990; O'Sullivan A, 'Some Misconceptions in the Current Housing Subsidy Debate', *Policy and Politics*, Volume 12, pp. 119-144, 1984; Hills, J, *Thirty-nine steps to housing finance reform*, Joseph Rowntree Foundation, 1991.

3 Recent measures of these elasticities can be found in Bramley G, Bartlett W, Franklin A and Lambert C, *op. cit*, 1990.

4 See: Bartlett W, 'A Note on Calculating Mortgage Interest Tax Relief', Bristol Case Study Team Working Paper.

5 Wilcox S, *op. cit.*, 1991.

6 Taking the period 1982 to 1989 with 1989 as base year, general 1982 prices had to be inflated by 38.8 per cent to bring them up to 1989 values. In the same period for the housing market, average house prices had to increase by an equivalent of 118.8 per cent. The Inland Revenue weighting implies, of course, a 100 per cent increase. The RPI is the correct measure to use for capital gains in general.

7 Forrest R and Murie A, *Selling the Welfare State: The Privatisation of Public Housing*, Routledge, 1991.

8 See Gibb K, *The Community Charge and Local Government Finance*, Centre for Housing Research Discussion Paper 20, University of Glasgow, 1988; and Coopers and Lybrand Deloitte, *Alternatives to the Community Charge*, Joseph Rowntree Foundation, 1990.

Chapter 6

Hills, J, *op. cit.*, Joseph Rowntree Foundation, 1991.

Appendix 1

Maclennan D, 'Some Thoughts on the Nature and Purpose of Urban House Price Studies', *Urban Studies*, 14, pp. 59-71, 1971; Quigley J, 'What have we Learned about Urban Housing Markets?' in Mieszkowski, P and Strazheim, M (eds): *Current Issues in Urban Economics*, John Hopkins Press, Baltimore, 1979; and Rosen S, 'Hedonic Prices and Implicit Markets: Product Differentiation and Pure Competition', *Journal of Political Economy*, 82, pp. 34-55, 1974.

About the authors

Duncan Maclennan

is the Mactaggart Professor of Land Economics and Finance at the University of Glasgow, where he is also Director of the Centre for Housing Research. His research interests in housing economics and finance, urban regeneration and social housing have resulted in a range of advisory positions at OECD (Paris), the Scottish office, Department of the Environment and other bodies. He is currently Chairman of the National Steering Committee for Care and Repair in Scotland and a member of the Board of Scottish Homes.

Kenneth Gibb

is a Research Fellow, funded by the ESRC, at the Centre for Housing Research. His research interests are in the economic aspects of housing markets and tax policies in relation to the housing system.

Alison More

is a Research Fellow at the Centre. A graduate of the Universities of Loughborough and Glasgow, she worked as a Development Officer in a housing association and subsequently in posts related to finance at the Scottish Federation of Housing Associations and Scottish Homes.